BIG-NOTE PIANO

TAYLOR SWIFT

ISBN 978-1-4950-1122-1

HAL•LEONARD®
CORPORATION
7777 W. BLUEMOUND RD. P.O. BOX 13819 MILWAUKEE, WI 53213

For all works contained herein:
Unauthorized copying, arranging, adapting, recording, Internet posting, public performance,
or other distribution of the printed music in this publication is an infringement of copyright.
Infringers are liable under the law.

Visit Hal Leonard Online at
www.halleonard.com

WELCOME TO NEW YORK

Words and Music by TAYLOR SWIFT
and RYAN TEDDER

Moderate Pop

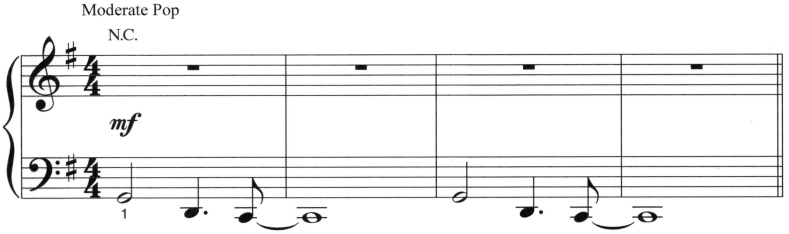

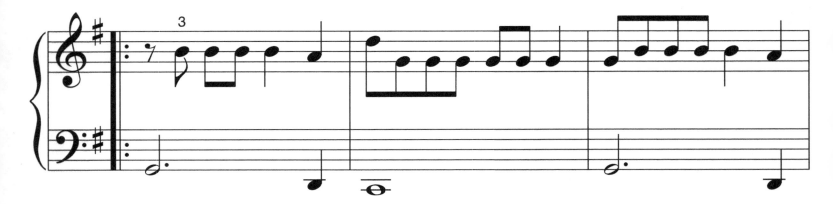

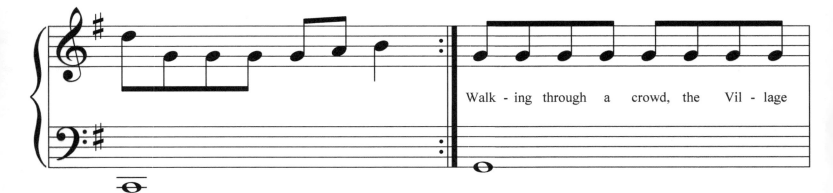

Walk-ing through a crowd, the Vil-lage

is a-glow, ka-lei-do-scope of loud heart-beats un-der coats.

Copyright © 2014 Sony/ATV Music Publishing LLC, Taylor Swift Music and Write Me A Song Publishing
All Rights on behalf of Sony/ATV Music Publishing LLC and Taylor Swift Music Administered by Sony/ATV Music Publishing LLC, 424 Church Street, Suite 1200, Nashville, TN 37219
All Rights on behalf of Write Me A Song Publishing Administered Worldwide by Kobalt Music Publishing America, Inc.
International Copyright Secured   All Rights Reserved

Ev-'ry-bod-y here want-ed some-thing more. Search-ing for a sound we had-n't

heard be-fore. And it said: Wel-come to New York, it's been wait-ing for you.

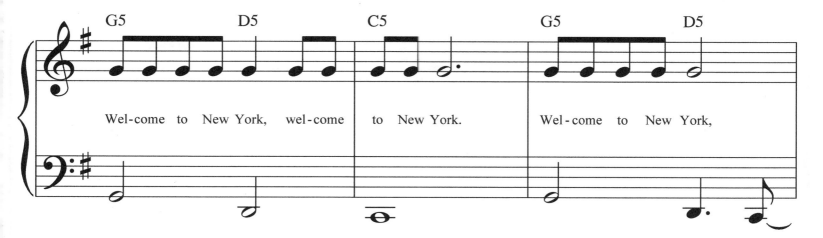

Wel-come to New York, wel-come to New York. Wel-come to New York,

it's been wait-ing for you. Wel-come to New York, wel-come to New York.

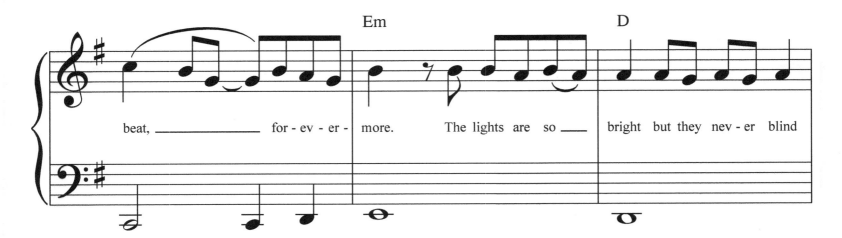

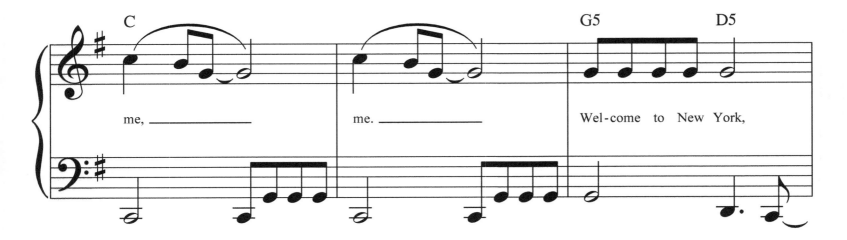

When we first dropped our bags on a- part-ment floors,

took our bro-ken hearts, put them in a drawer. Ev-'ry-bod-y here was some-one

D.S. al Coda

else be-fore. And you can watch who you want, boys and boys and girls and girls.

CODA

Like an-y great love, it keeps you guess-ing. Like an-y real love,

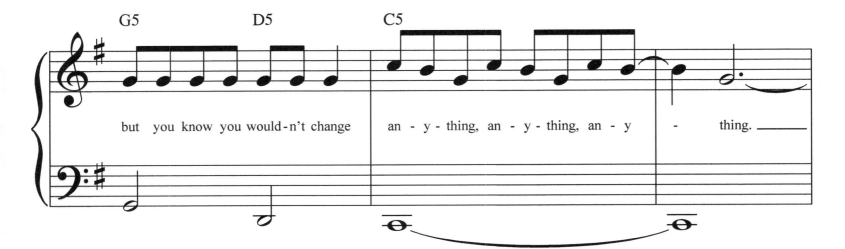

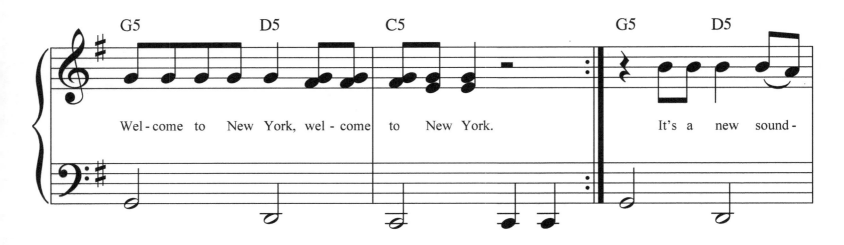

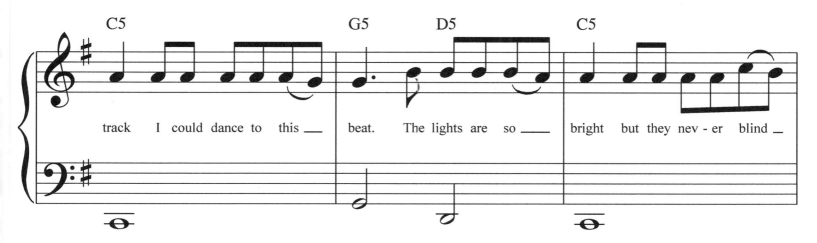

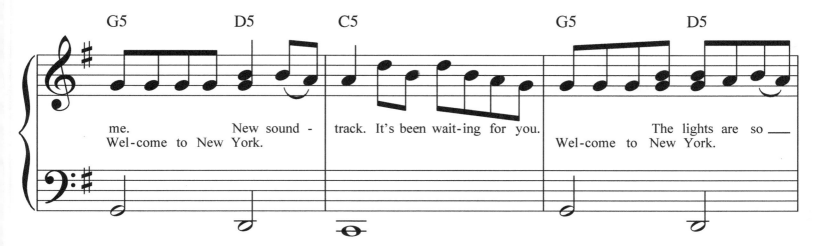

BLANK SPACE

Words and Music by TAYLOR SWIFT,
MAX MARTIN and SHELLBACK

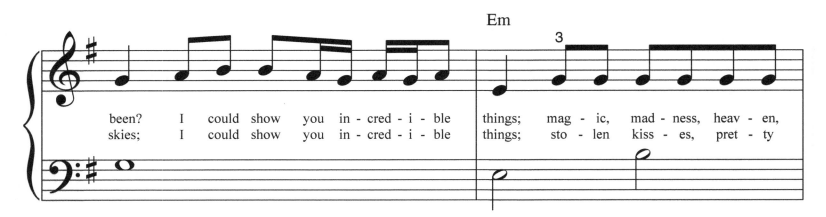

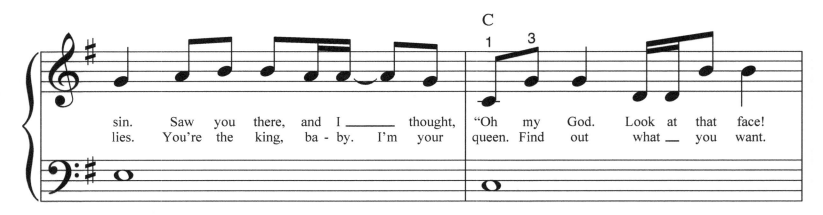

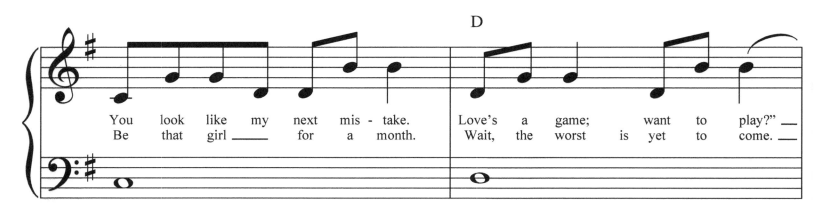

Copyright © 2014 Sony/ATV Music Publishing LLC, Taylor Swift Music and MXM
All Rights on behalf of Sony/ATV Music Publishing LLC and Taylor Swift Music Administered by Sony/ATV Music Publishing LLC, 424 Church Street, Suite 1200, Nashville, TN 37219
All Rights on behalf of MXM Administered Worldwide by Kobalt Songs Music Publishing
International Copyright Secured All Rights Reserved

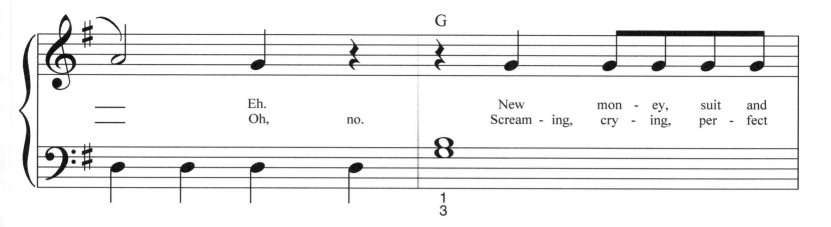

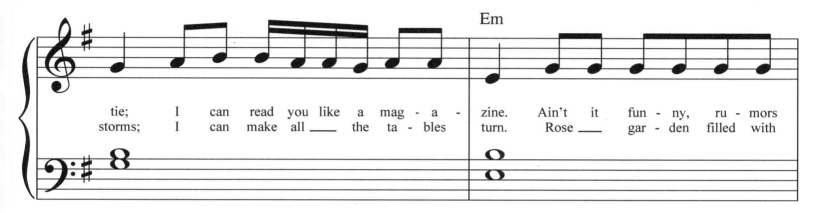

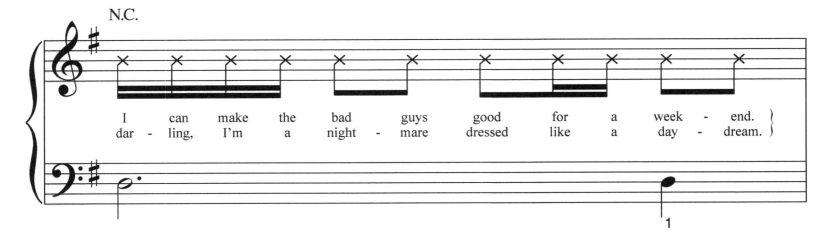

I can make the bad guys good for a week - end.
dar - ling, I'm a night - mare dressed like a day - dream.

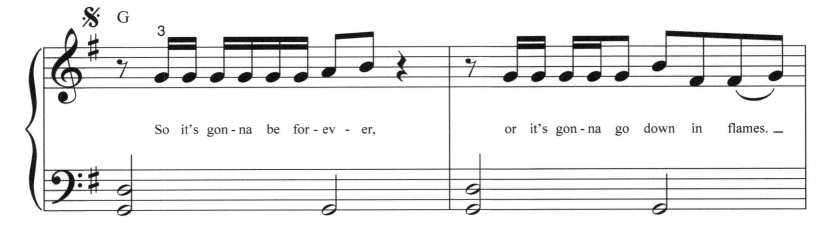

So it's gon - na be for - ev - er, or it's gon - na go down in flames. __

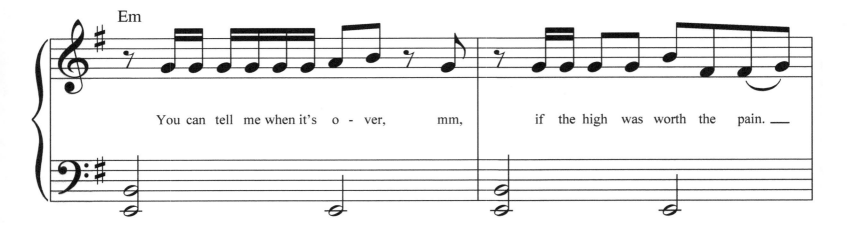

You can tell me when it's o - ver, mm, if the high was worth the pain. __

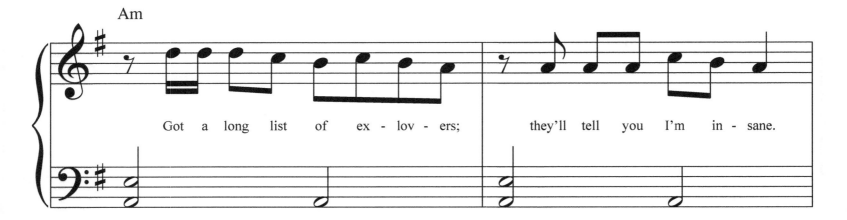

Got a long list of ex - lov - ers; they'll tell you I'm in - sane.

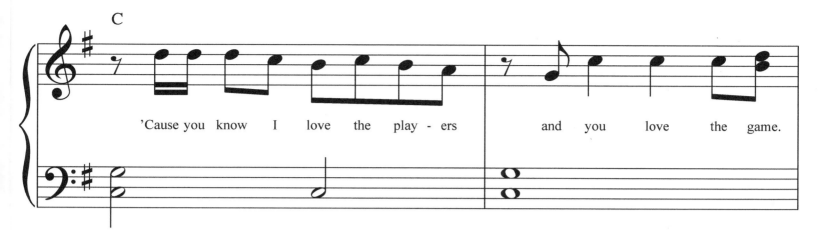

'Cause you know I love the play - ers and you love the game.

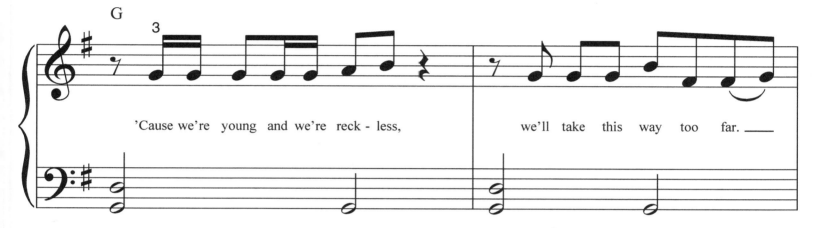

'Cause we're young and we're reck - less, we'll take this way too far. ___

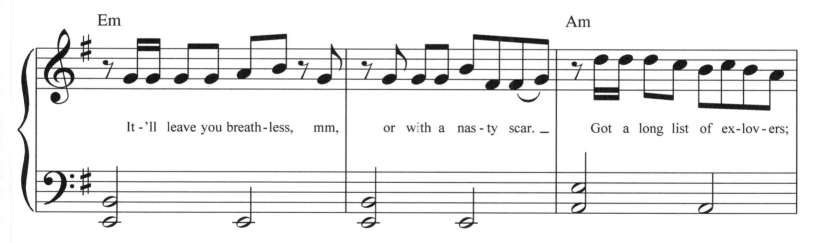

It -'ll leave you breath-less, mm, or with a nas - ty scar. _ Got a long list of ex - lov - ers;

they'll tell you I'm in - sane. But I've got a blank space, ba - by, and I'll write your name.

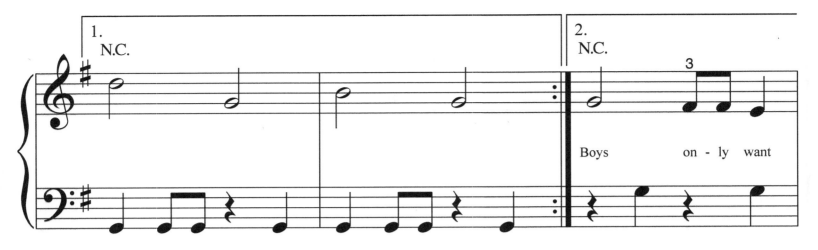

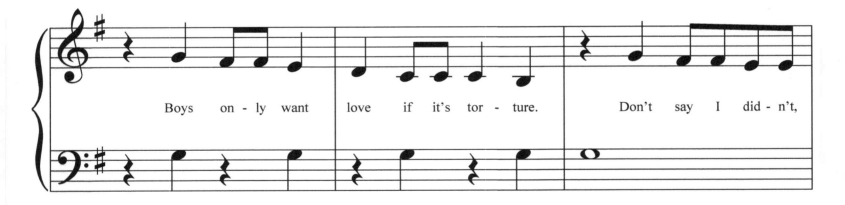

STYLE

Words and Music by TAYLOR SWIFT,
MAX MARTIN, SHELLBACK
and ALI PAYAMI

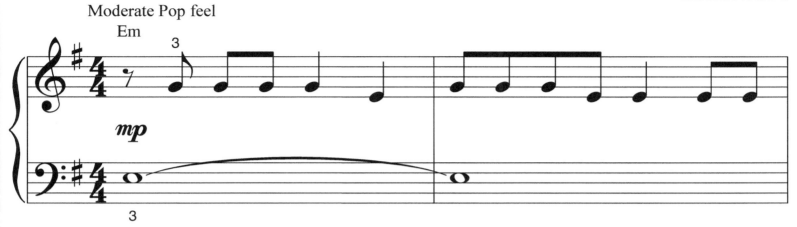

Copyright © 2014 Sony/ATV Music Publishing LLC, Taylor Swift Music, MXM, Warner/Chappell Music Scandinavia AB and Wolf Cousins
All Rights on behalf of Sony/ATV Music Publishing LLC and Taylor Swift Music Administered by Sony/ATV Music Publishing LLC, 424 Church Street, Suite 1200, Nashville, TN 37219
All Rights on behalf of MXM Administered Worldwide by Kobalt Songs Music Publishing
All Rights on behalf of Warner/Chappell Music Scandinavia AB and Wolf Cousins in the U.S. and Canada Administered by WB Music Corp.
International Copyright Secured   All Rights Reserved

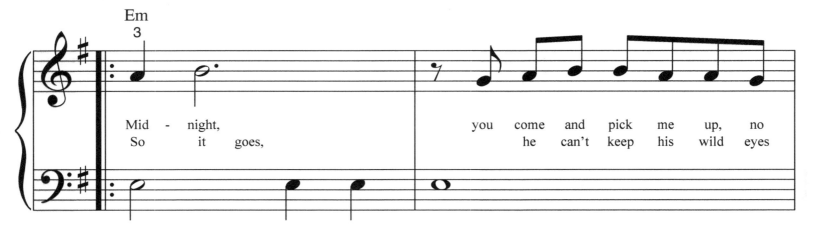

Midnight, you come and pick me up, no
So it goes, he can't keep his wild eyes

head - lights. Long drive,
on the road. Takes me home,

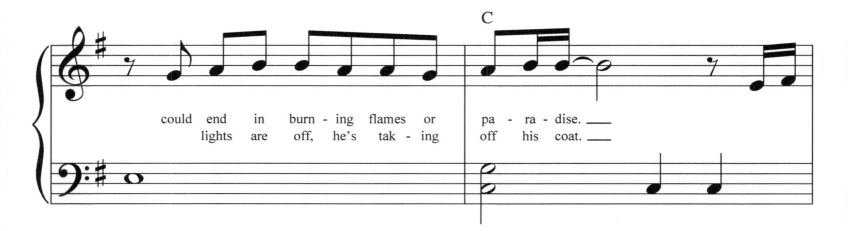

could end in burn - ing flames or pa - ra - dise. ___
lights are off, he's tak - ing off his coat. ___

Fade in - to view, ___ oh, it's
I say I heard, ___ oh, that

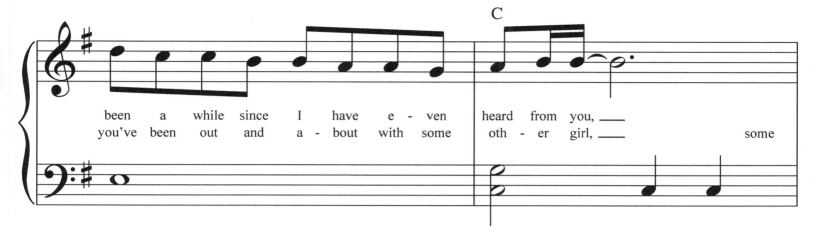

been a while since I have e - ven heard from you, ___
you've been out and a - bout with some oth - er girl, ___ some

heard from you. ___ And I should just tell you to leave 'cause I
oth - er girl. ___ He says, "What you've heard is true, but I

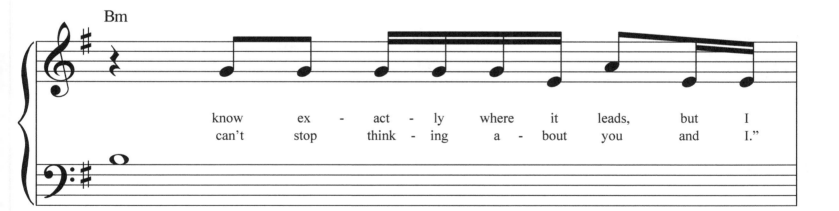

know ex - act - ly where it leads, but I
can't stop think - ing a - bout you and I."

watch us go round and round each time. ___ } You got that
I said, "I've been there too, a few times." } You got that

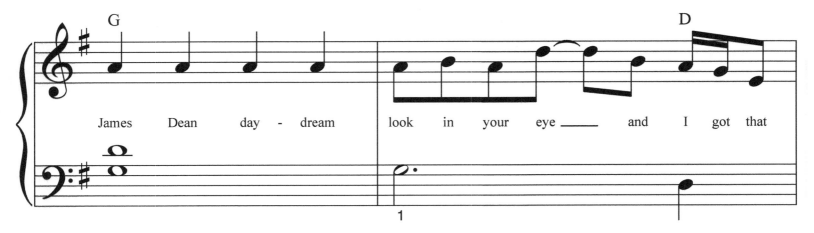

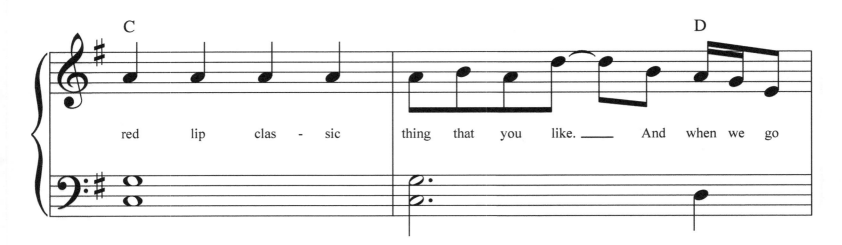

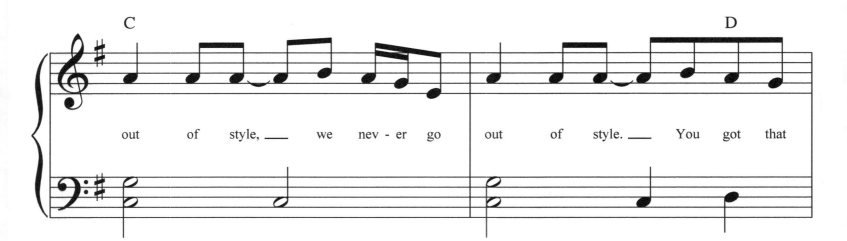

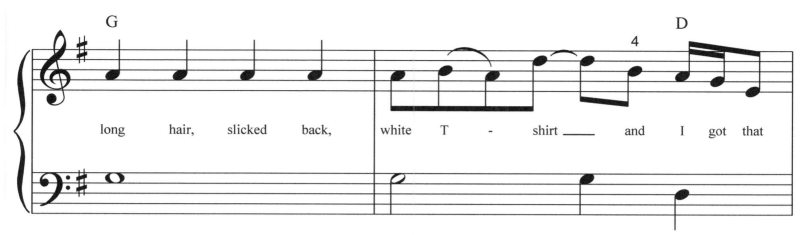

long hair, slicked back, white T - shirt ___ and I got that

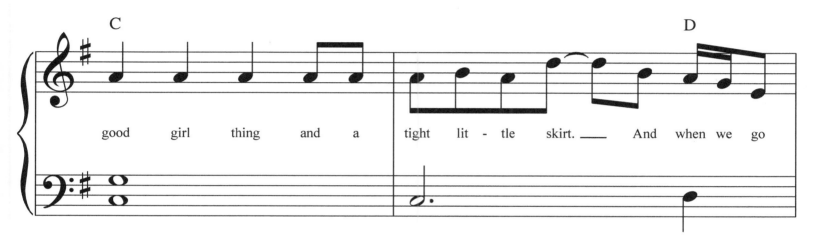

good girl thing and a tight lit - tle skirt. ___ And when we go

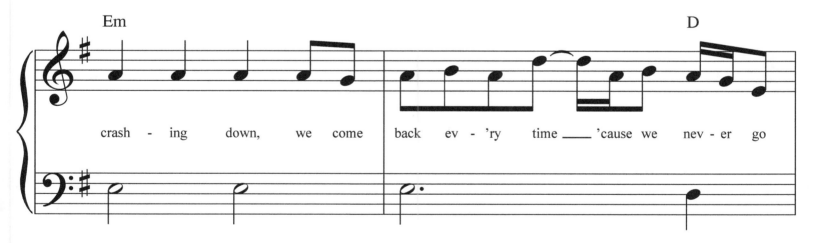

crash - ing down, we come back ev - 'ry time ___ 'cause we nev - er go

out of style, ___ we nev - er go out of style. ___

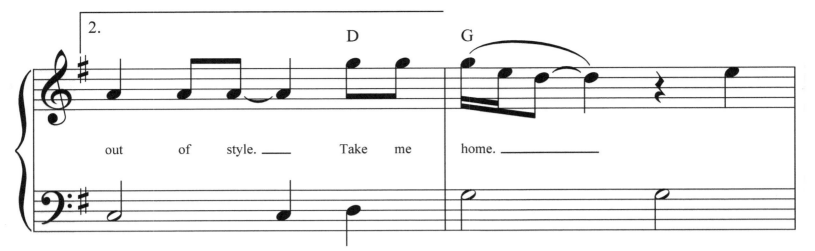

out of style.____ Take me home._____

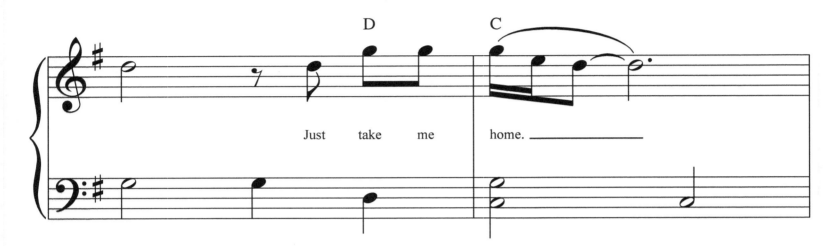

Just take me home._____

Oh,____ just take me home._____ Oh.____

Oh, you got that

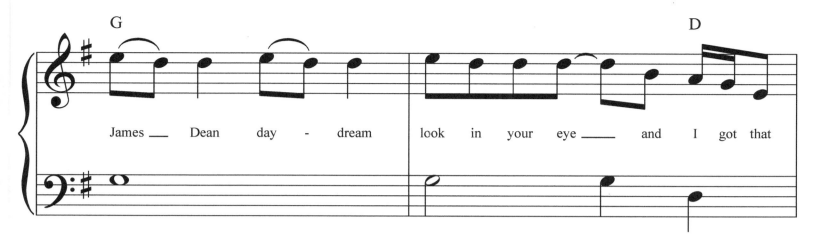

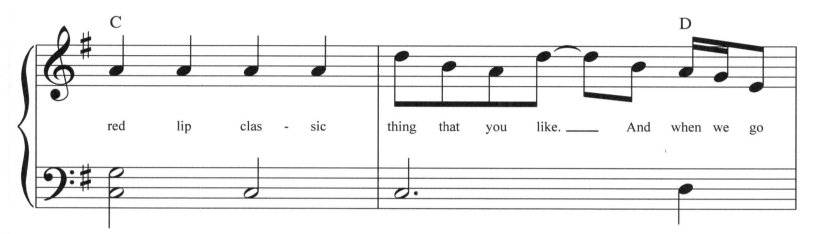

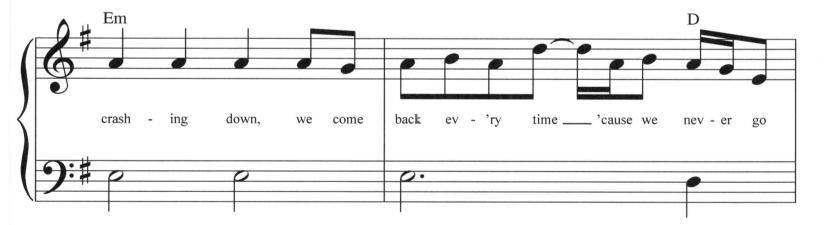

OUT OF THE WOODS

Words and Music by TAYLOR SWIFT
and JACK ANTONOFF

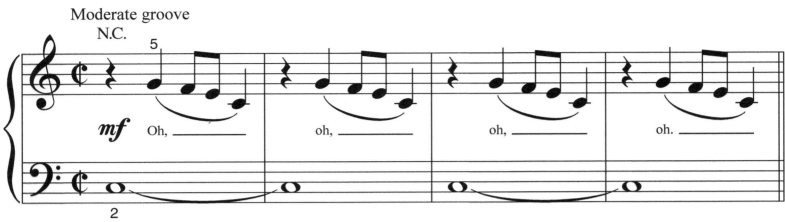

Copyright © 2014 Sony/ATV Music Publishing LLC, Taylor Swift Music and Ducky Donath Music
All Rights Administered by Sony/ATV Music Publishing LLC, 424 Church Street, Suite 1200, Nashville, TN 37219
International Copyright Secured   All Rights Reserved

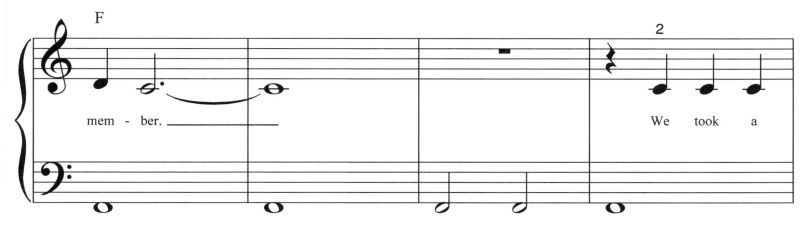

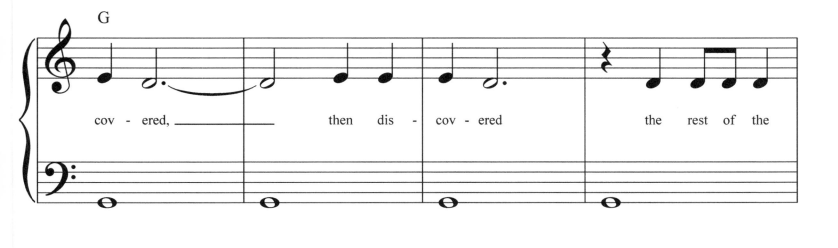

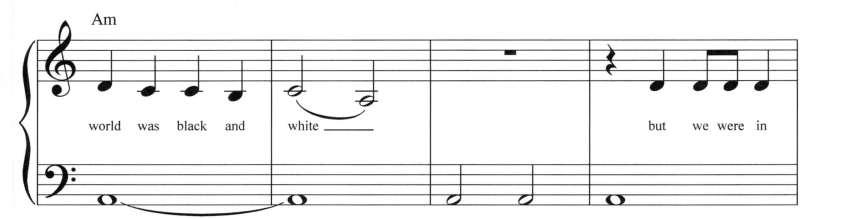

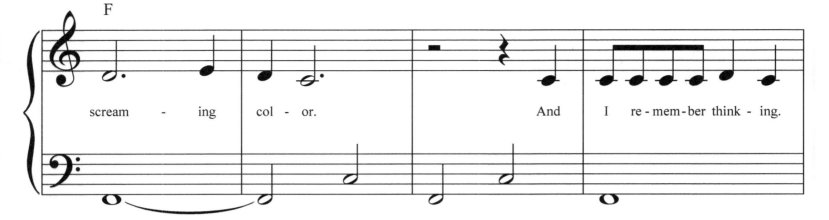

F

scream - ing col - or. And I re - mem - ber think - ing.

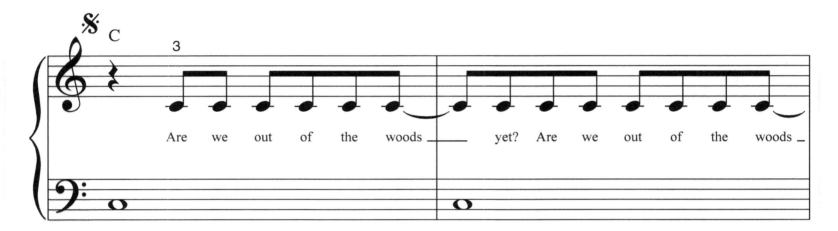

C 3

Are we out of the woods ___ yet? Are we out of the woods ___

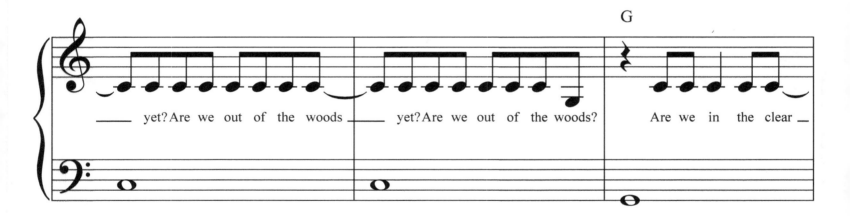

G

___ yet? Are we out of the woods ___ yet? Are we out of the woods? Are we in the clear ___

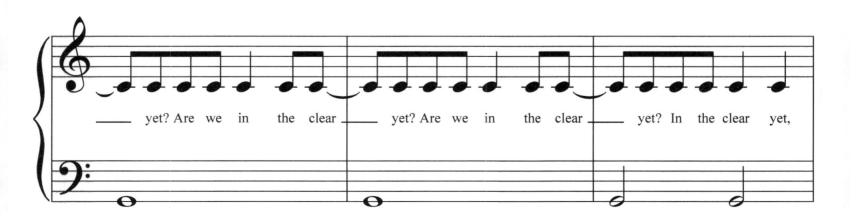

___ yet? Are we in the clear ___ yet? Are we in the clear ___ yet? In the clear yet,

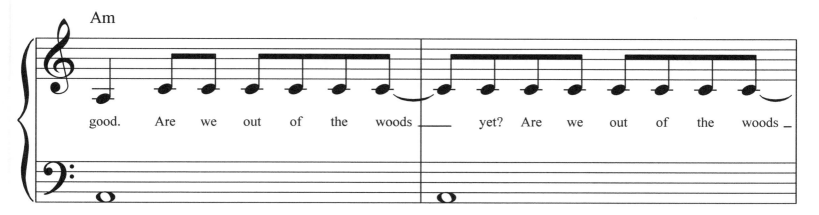

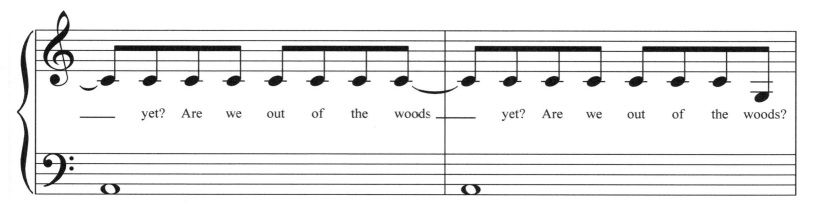

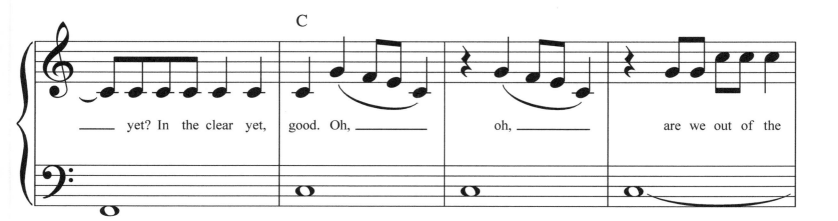

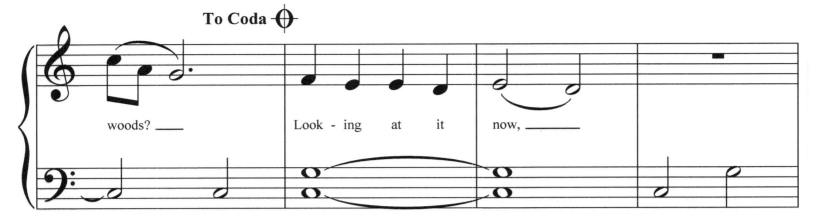

To Coda ⊕

woods? ___ Look - ing at it now, ___

G

last De - cem - ber, ___ last De - cem - ber.

Am

We were built to fall a - part, ___

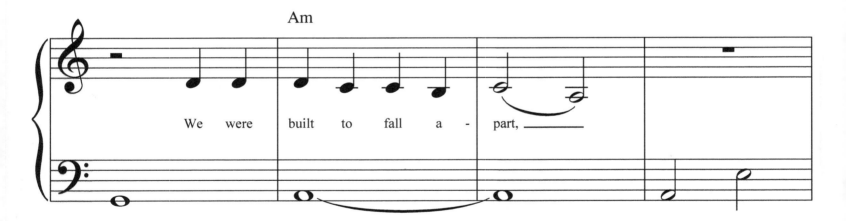

F

and fall back to - geth - er, back to - geth - er. Ooh, _

2

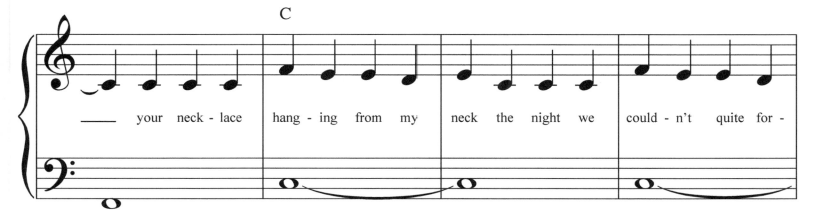

C

your neck - lace hang - ing from my neck the night we could - n't quite for -

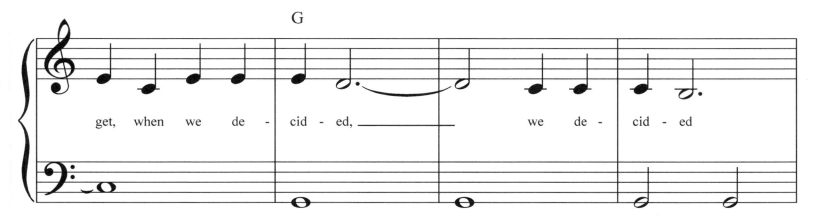

G

get, when we de - cid - ed, _____ we de - cid - ed

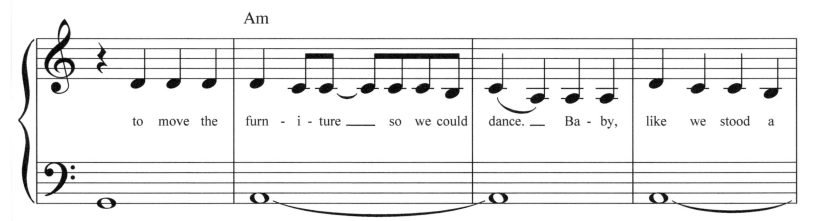

Am

to move the furn - i - ture ___ so we could dance. ___ Ba - by, like we stood a

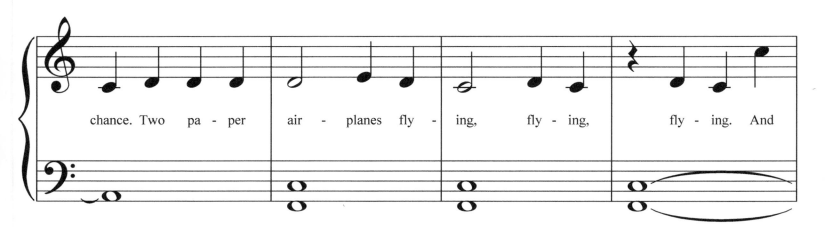

chance. Two pa - per air - planes fly - ing, fly - ing, fly - ing. And

D.S. al Coda

I re-mem-ber think-ing.

CODA

C

1

Re - mem - ber | when you hit the brakes too

G

soon? Twen - ty | stitch-es in the hos-pi-tal | room. When you start-ed | cry-ing ba-by, I did

Am

too. But when the sun came | up, I was look-ing at | you. Re-mem-ber | when we could-n't take the

F

heat? I walked | out. I said, "I'm set-ting you | free." But the mon-sters

turned out to be just trees. When the sun came up, you were look-ing at me. _____

_____ You were look-ing at me. _____

Oh, _____ you were look-ing at me. __ Are we out of the woods __

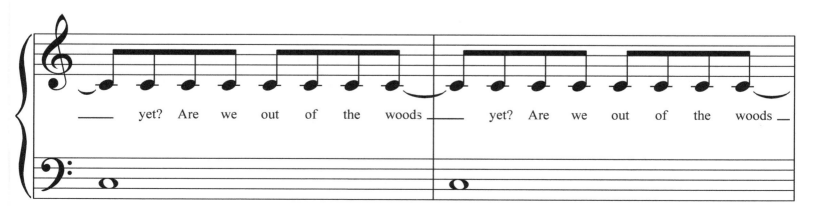

_____ yet? Are we out of the woods _____ yet? Are we out of the woods __

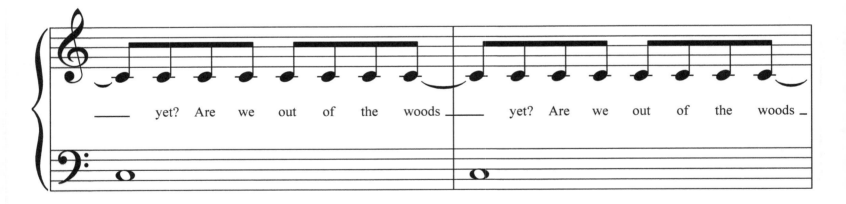

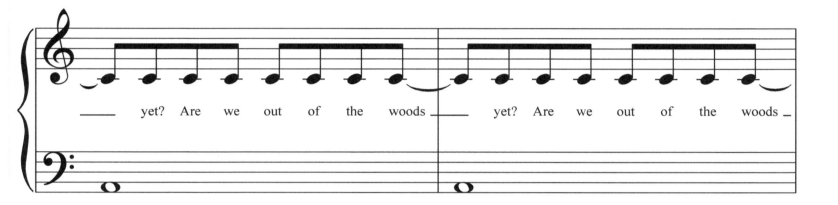

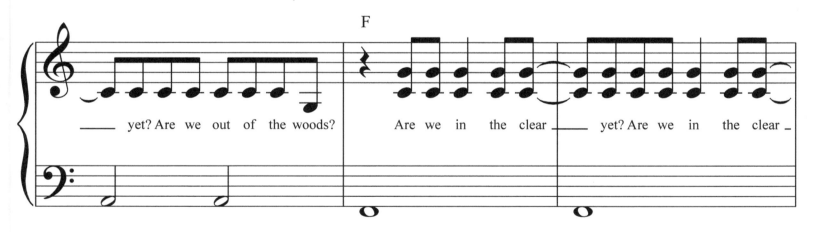

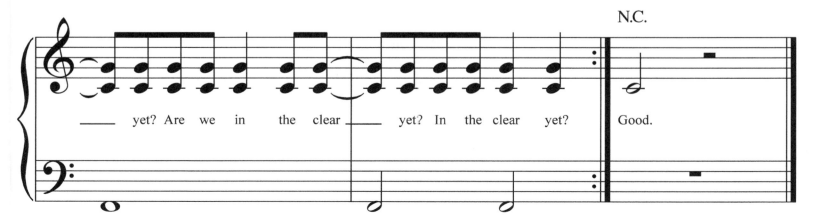

ALL YOU HAD TO DO WAS STAY

Words and Music by TAYLOR SWIFT
and MAX MARTIN

Moderate Groove

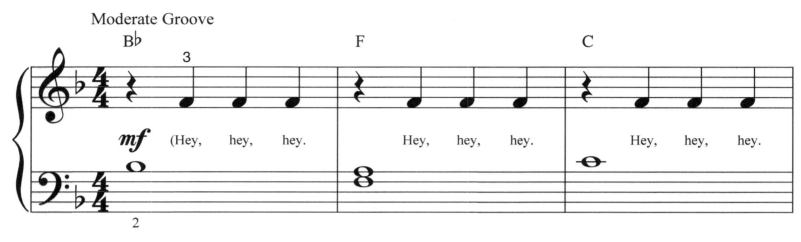

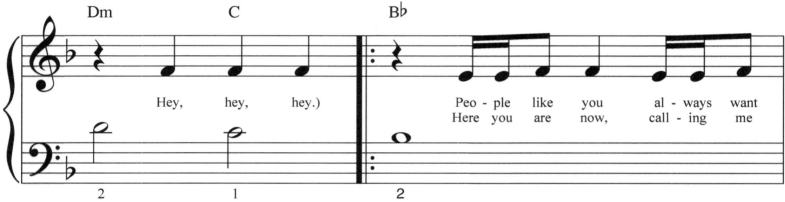

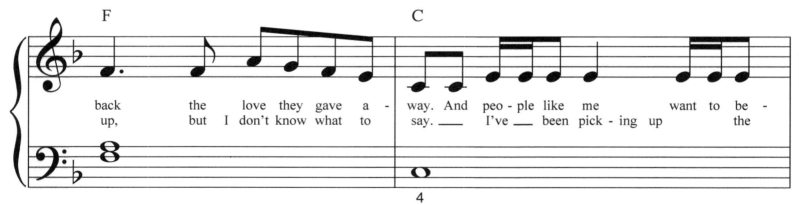

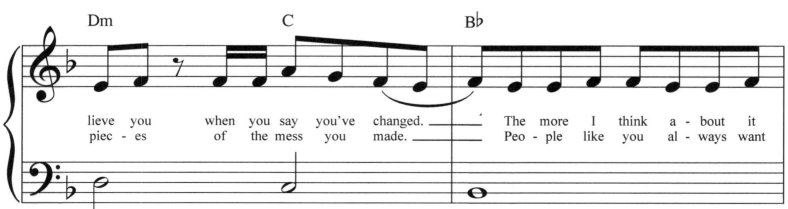

Copyright © 2014 Sony/ATV Music Publishing LLC, Taylor Swift Music and MXM
All Rights on behalf of Sony/ATV Music Publishing LLC and Taylor Swift Music Administered by Sony/ATV Music Publishing LLC, 424 Church Street, Suite 1200, Nashville, TN 37219
All Rights on behalf of MXM Administered Worldwide by Kobalt Songs Music Publishing
International Copyright Secured   All Rights Reserved

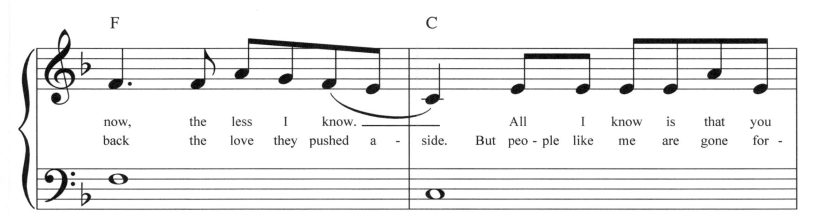

now,   the   less   I   know. _____   All   I   know   is   that   you
back   the   love they pushed a - side. But peo - ple like   me   are   gone   for -

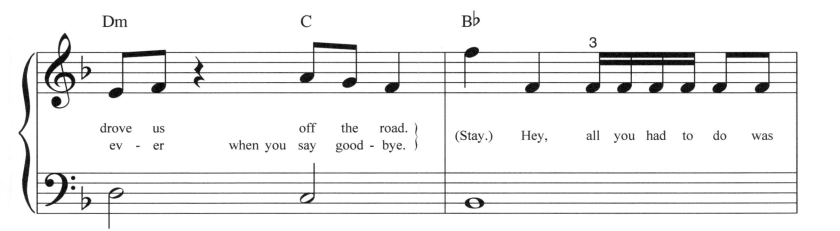

drove   us   off   the   road.   (Stay.)   Hey,   all   you   had   to   do   was
ev -   er   when you say   good - bye.

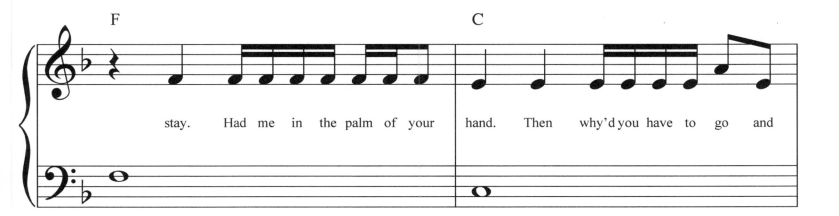

stay.   Had   me   in   the   palm of your   hand.   Then   why'd you have to   go   and

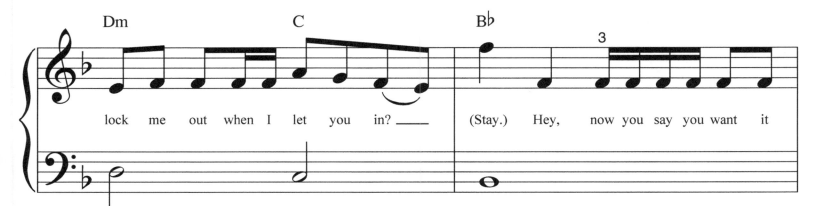

lock   me   out   when I   let   you   in? _____   (Stay.)   Hey,   now you say you want   it

back, now that it's just too late. Well, it could-'ve been eas - y. ___

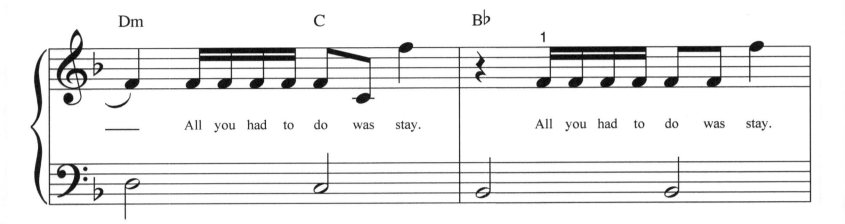

___ All you had to do was stay. All you had to do was stay.

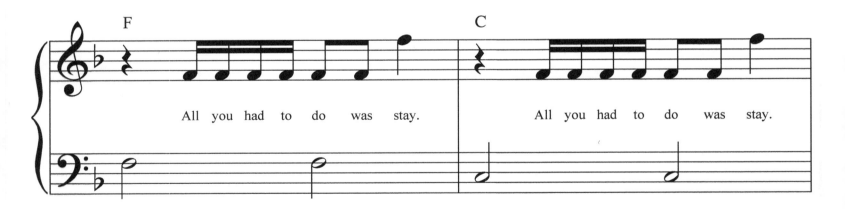

All you had to do was stay. All you had to do was stay.

All you had to do was stay. (Stay. Stay.) Let me re - mind you,

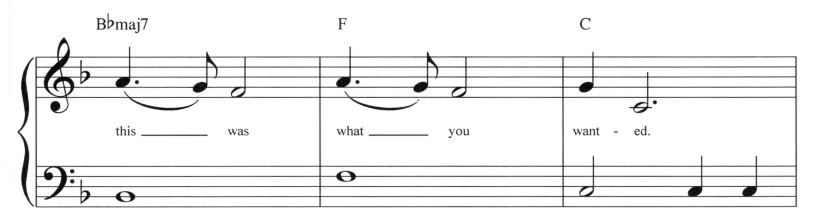

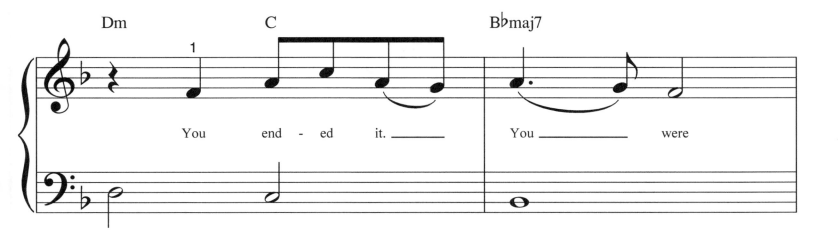

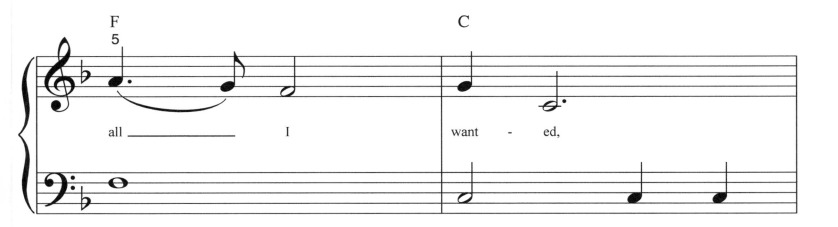

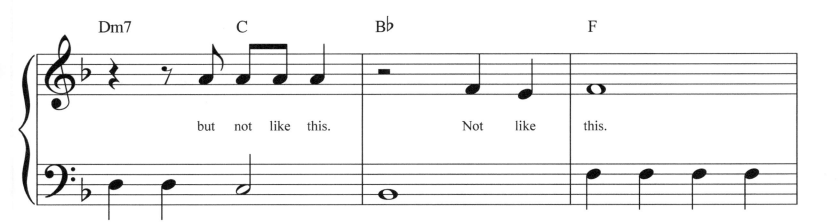

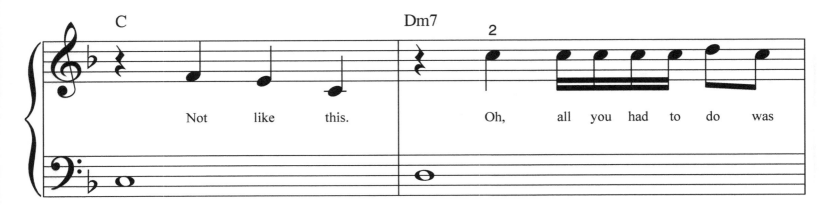

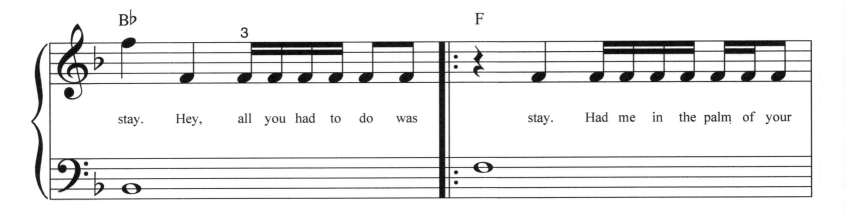

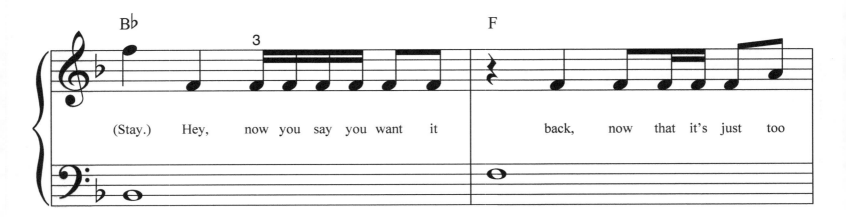

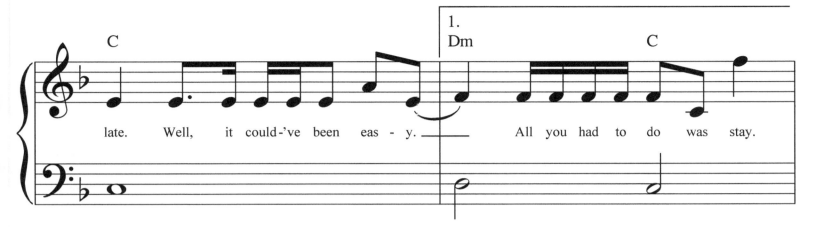

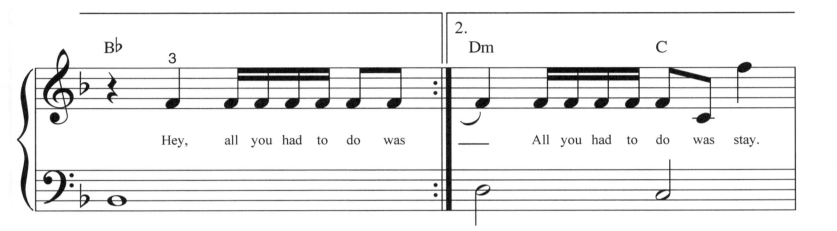

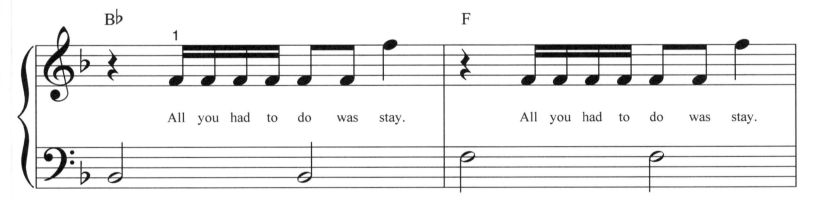

SHAKE IT OFF

Words and Music by TAYLOR SWIFT,
MAX MARTIN and SHELLBACK

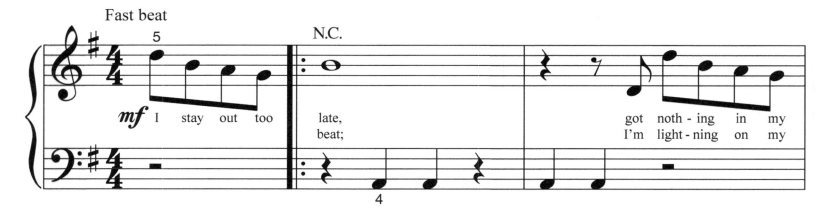

Copyright © 2014 Sony/ATV Music Publishing LLC, Taylor Swift Music and MXM
All Rights on behalf of Sony/ATV Music Publishing LLC and Taylor Swift Music Administered by Sony/ATV Music Publishing LLC, 424 Church Street, Suite 1200, Nashville, TN 37219
All Rights on behalf of MXM Administered Worldwide by Kobalt Songs Music Publishing
International Copyright Secured   All Rights Reserved

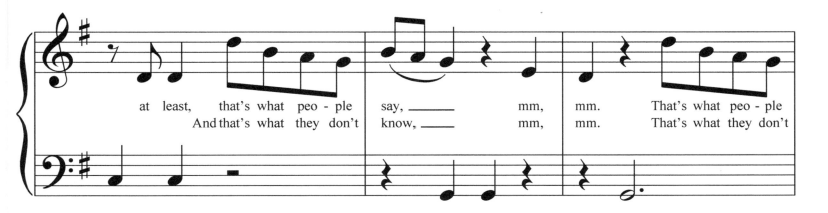

at least, that's what peo - ple say, _____ mm, mm. That's what peo - ple
And that's what they don't know, _____ mm, mm. That's what they don't

say, _____ mm, mm. But I keep cruis - ing;
know, _____ mm, mm. But I keep cruis - ing;

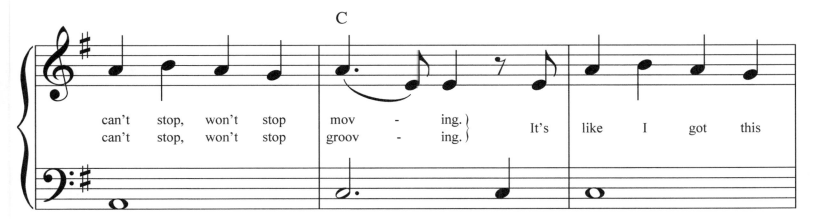

can't stop, won't stop mov - ing. } It's like I got this
can't stop, won't stop groov - ing. }

mu - sic in my mind say - ing, "It's gon - na be al -

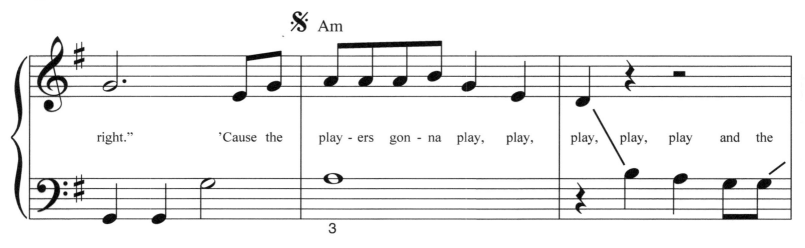

right."   'Cause the   play - ers gon - na play,   play,   play,   play,   play   and   the

hat - ers gon - na hate, hate,   hate, hate, hate, ba - by.   I'm just gon - na shake, shake,

shake, shake, shake;   I   shake it off,   I shake it   off.   Heart -

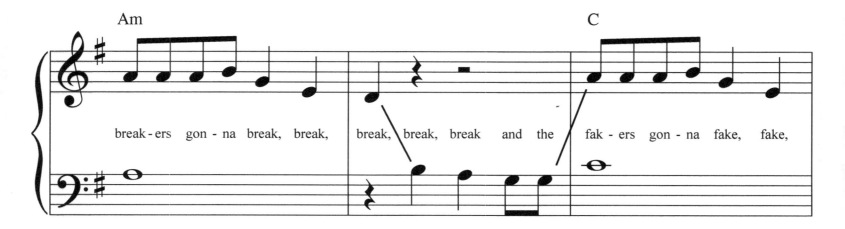

break - ers gon - na break, break,   break, break, break   and the   fak - ers gon - na fake, fake,

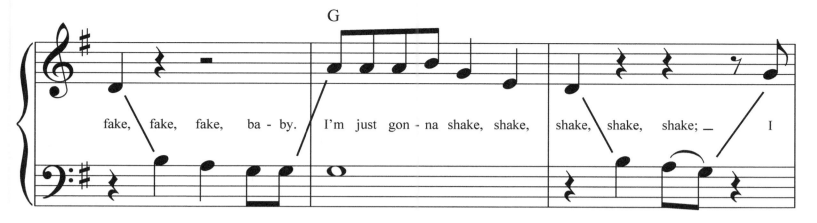

fake, fake, fake, ba - by. I'm just gon - na shake, shake, shake, shake, shake; _____ I

shake it off, I shake it off. I nev - er miss a off. I

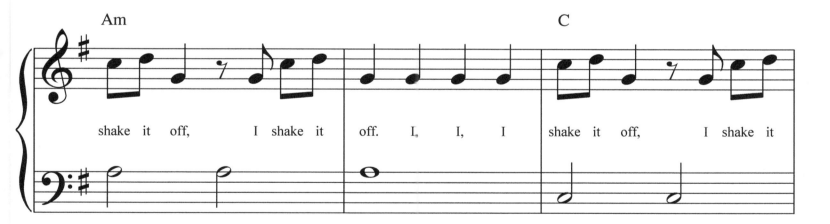

shake it off, I shake it off. I, I, I shake it off, I shake it

off. I, I, I shake it off, I shake it off. I, I, I

N.C.

shake it off, I shake it off. (Ooh, ___ ooh!)

1. *Spoken: (See additional lyrics)*
2. Rap: *(See additional lyrics)*

D.S. al Coda

Rap ends   Yeah,   oh. _____   'Cause   the

CODA

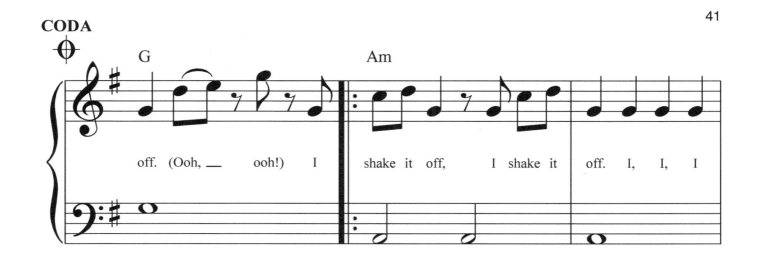

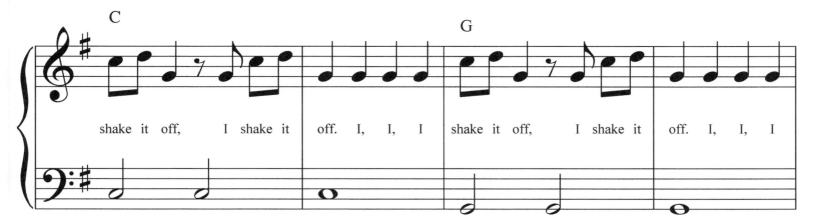

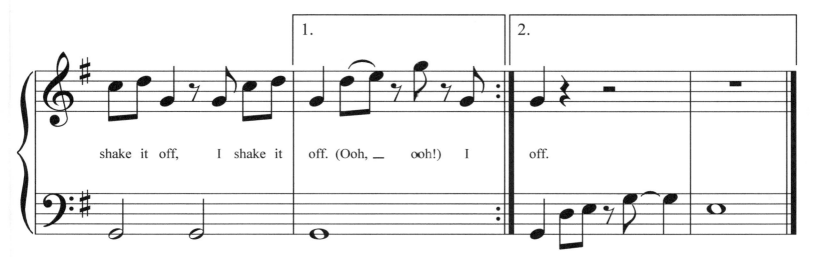

Additional Lyrics

Spoken: *Hey, hey, hey! Just think: While you've been getting*
Down and out about the liars and the dirty, dirty
Cheats of the world, you could've been getting down to
This. Sick. Beat!

Rap: My ex-man brought his new girlfriend.
She's like, "Oh, my god!" But I'm just gonna shake.
And to the fella over there with the hella good hair,
Won't you come on over, baby? We can shake, shake, shake.

I WISH YOU WOULD

Words and Music by TAYLOR SWIFT
and JACK ANTONOFF

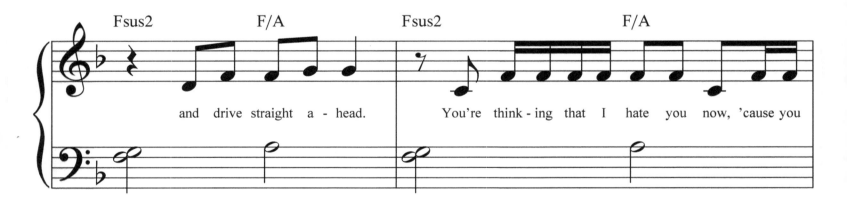

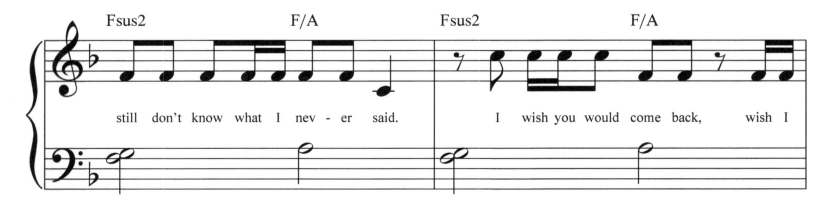

Copyright © 2014 Sony/ATV Music Publishing LLC, Taylor Swift Music and Ducky Donath Music
All Rights Administered by Sony/ATV Music Publishing LLC, 424 Church Street, Suite 1200, Nashville, TN 37219
International Copyright Secured All Rights Reserved

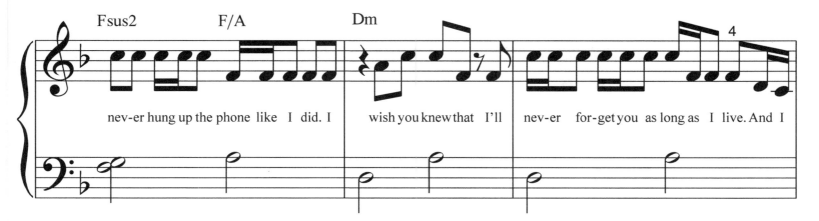

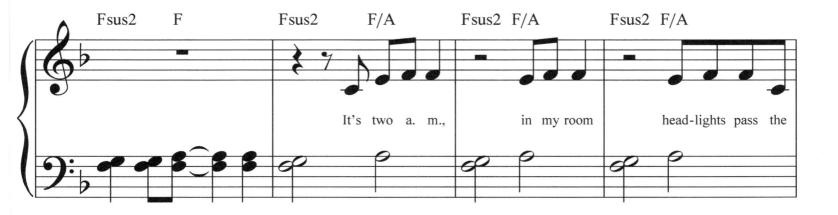

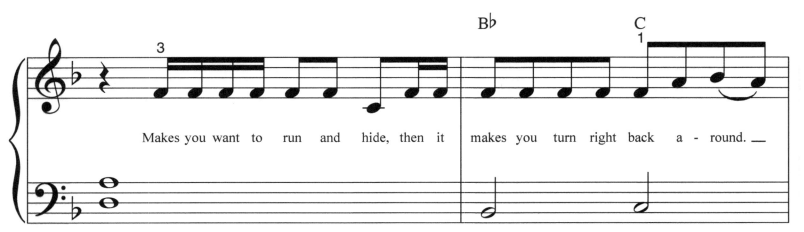

Makes you want to run and hide, then it makes you turn right back a - round. __

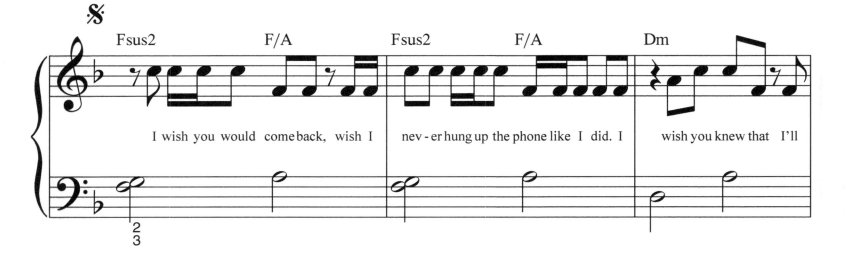

I wish you would come back, wish I nev - er hung up the phone like I did. I wish you knew that I'll

nev - er for - get you as long as I live. And I wish you were right here, right

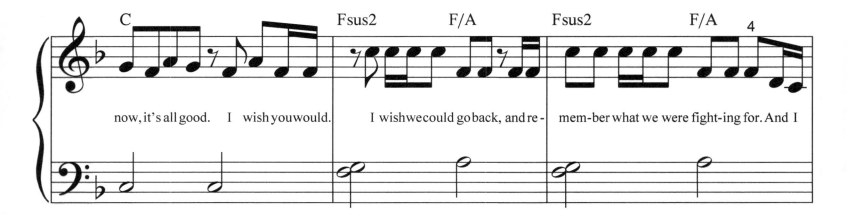

now, it's all good. I wish you would. I wish we could go back, and re - mem - ber what we were fight-ing for. And I

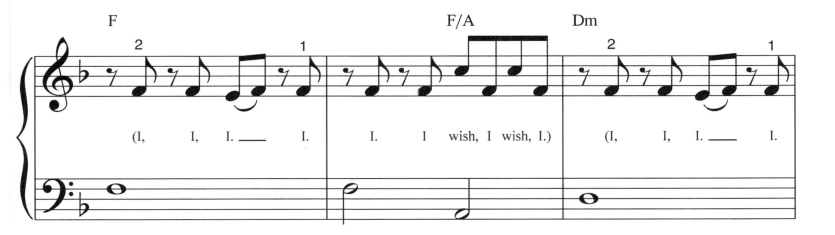

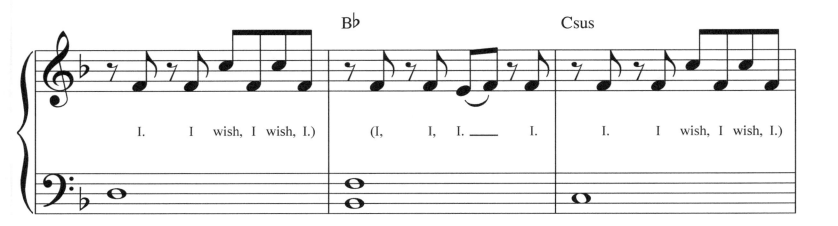

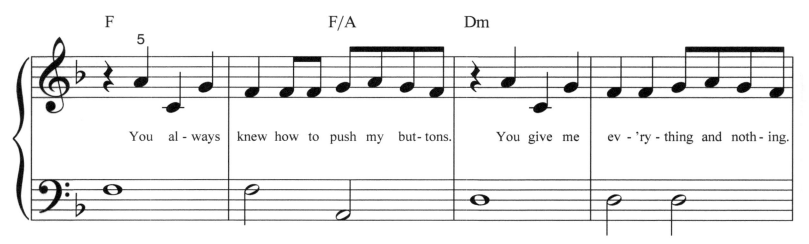

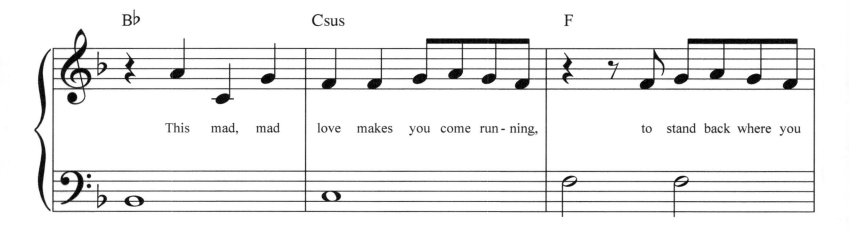

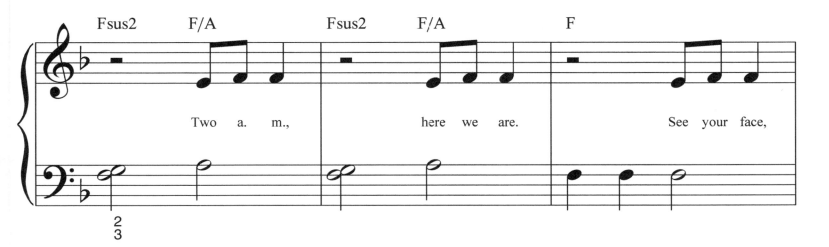

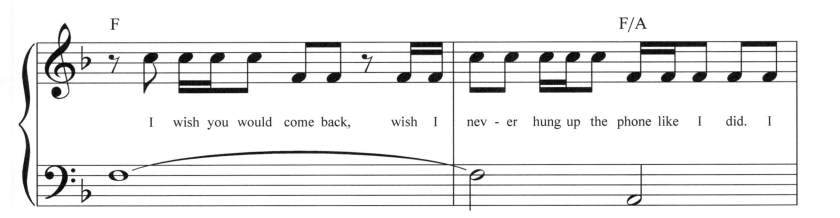

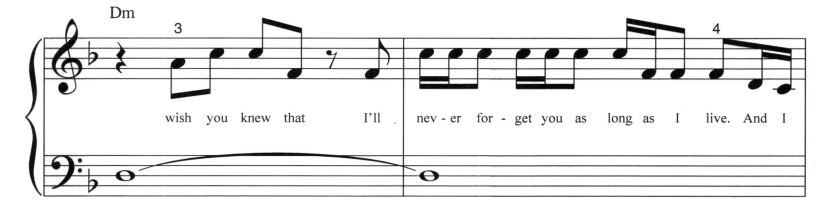

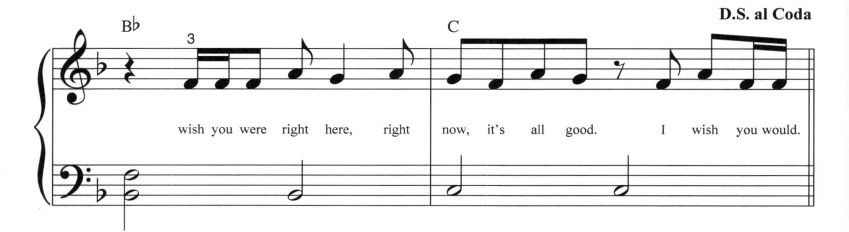

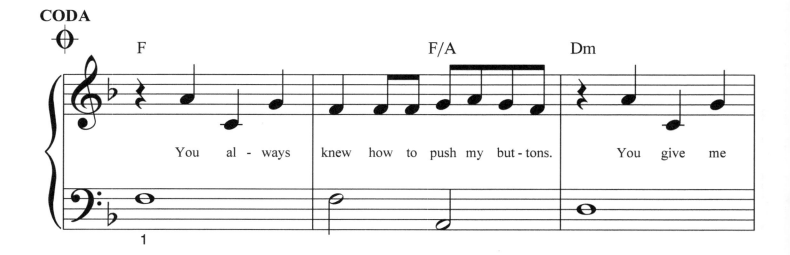

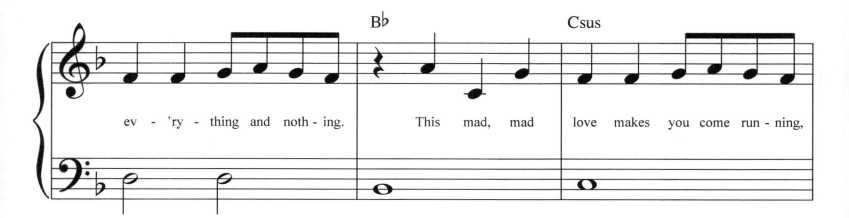

F   F/A

to stand back where you stood, I wish you would. ___ I wish you would. ___

Dm

___ I wish you would. ___ I wish you would. ___

B♭   Csus   N.C.

___ (I,   I wish, I wish, I.)   (I,   I,   I. ___   I.

I.   I wish, I wish, I.)   (I,   I,   I. ___   I.   I.   I wish.) I wish you would.

BAD BLOOD

Words and Music by TAYLOR SWIFT,
MAX MARTIN and SHELLBACK

Moderately, in 2

'Cause ba - by, now we got bad _____ blood. You know, it
Now we got prob - lems, and I don't

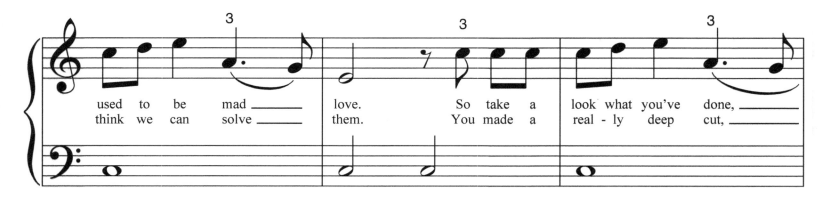

used to be mad _____ love. So take a look what you've done, _____
think we can solve _____ them. You made a real - ly deep cut, _____

_____ 'cause ba - by, now we got bad _____ blood. Hey!
and ba - by, now we got bad _____ blood. Hey!

F   C   G

Did you have to do this? I was think - ing that
Did you think we'd be fine? Still got scars on my

Copyright © 2014 Sony/ATV Music Publishing LLC, Taylor Swift Music and MXM
All Rights on behalf of Sony/ATV Music Publishing LLC and Taylor Swift Music Administered by Sony/ATV Music Publishing LLC, 424 Church Street, Suite 1200, Nashville, TN 37219
All Rights on behalf of MXM Administered Worldwide by Kobalt Songs Music Publishing
International Copyright Secured   All Rights Reserved

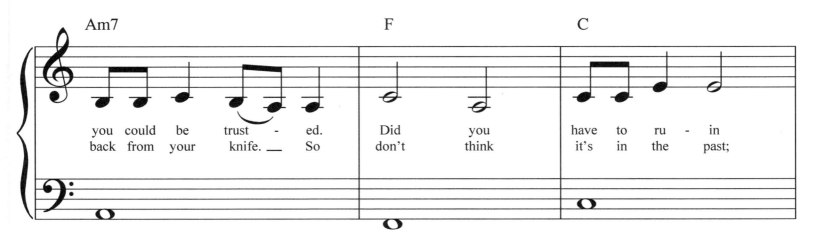

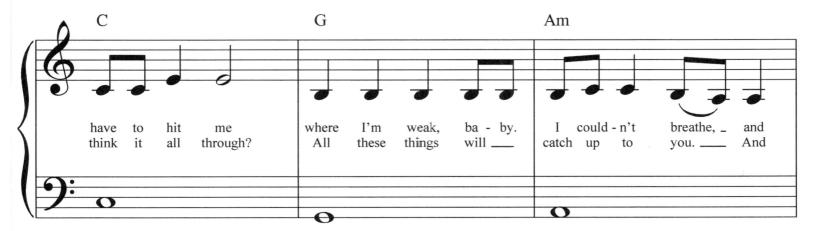

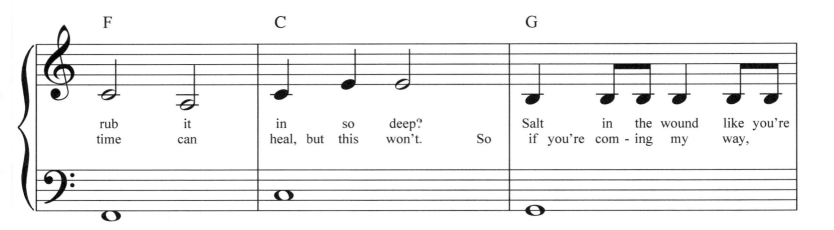

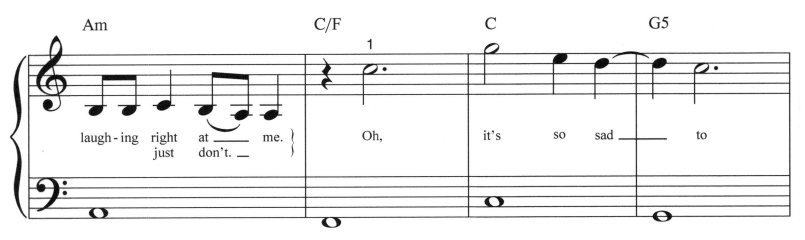

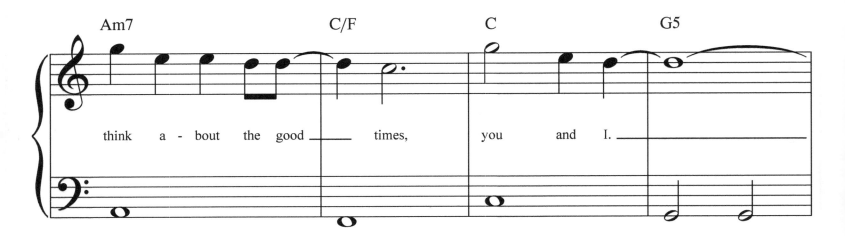

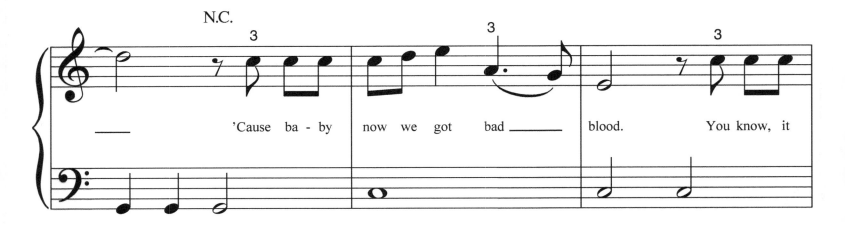

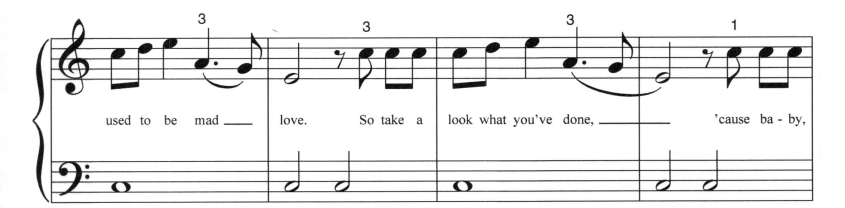

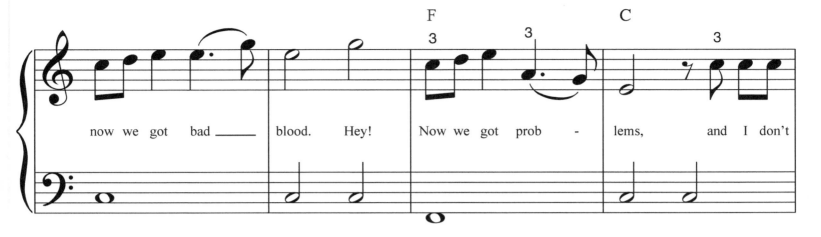

now we got bad _____ blood. Hey! Now we got prob - lems, and I don't

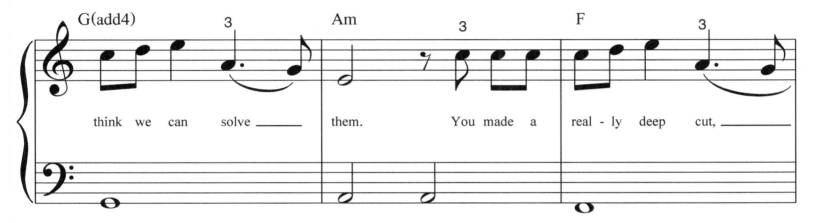

think we can solve _____ them. You made a real - ly deep cut, _____

_____ and ba - by, now we got bad _____ blood. Hey!

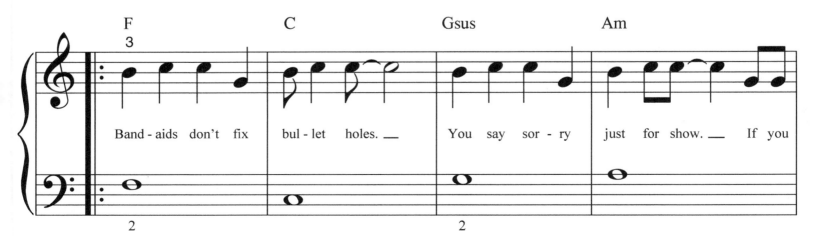

Band - aids don't fix bul - let holes. _____ You say sor - ry just for show. _____ If you

live like that, you live with ghosts. —

Mm, — if you love like that, — blood runs cold.

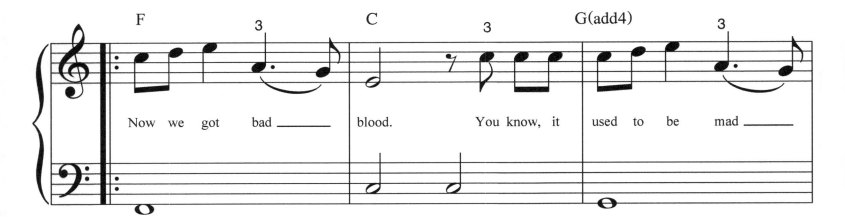

Now we got bad _____ blood. You know, it used to be mad _____ love.

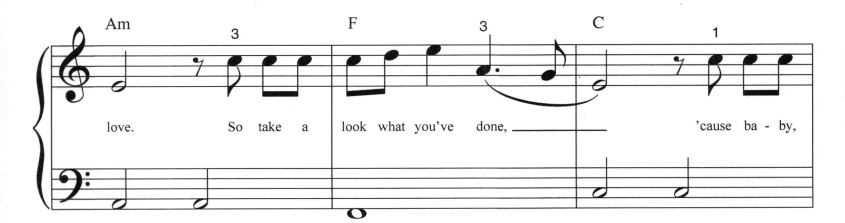

love. So take a look what you've done, _____ 'cause ba - by,

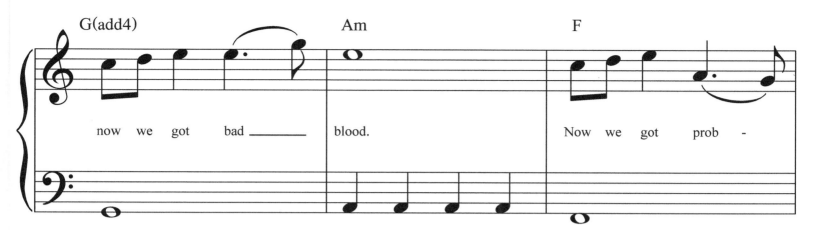

WILDEST DREAMS

Words and Music by TAYLOR SWIFT,
MAX MARTIN and SHELLBACK

Moderate Ballad

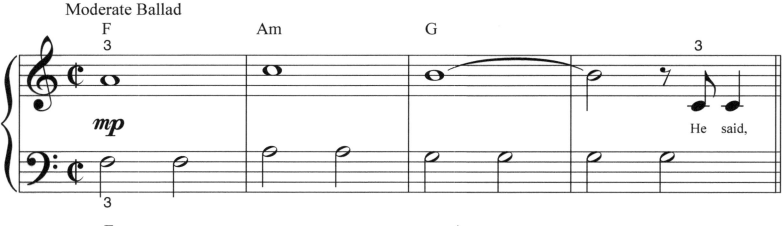

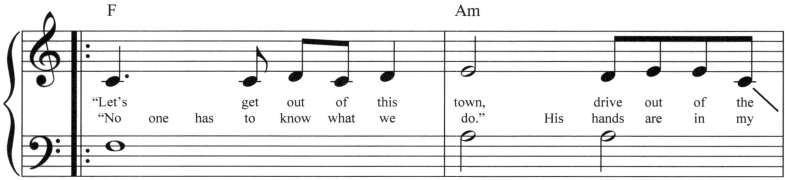

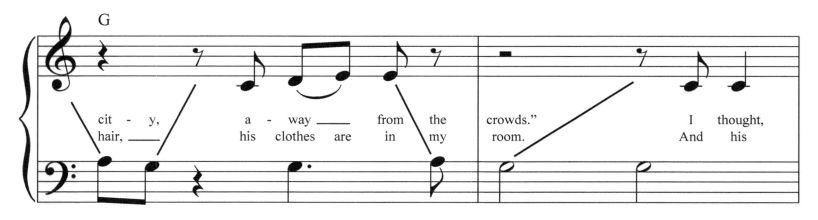

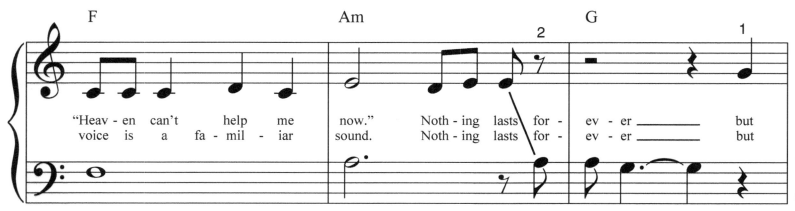

Copyright © 2014 Sony/ATV Music Publishing LLC, Taylor Swift Music and MXM
All Rights on behalf of Sony/ATV Music Publishing LLC and Taylor Swift Music Administered by Sony/ATV Music Publishing LLC, 424 Church Street, Suite 1200, Nashville, TN 37219
All Rights on behalf of MXM Administered Worldwide by Kobalt Songs Music Publishing
International Copyright Secured   All Rights Reserved

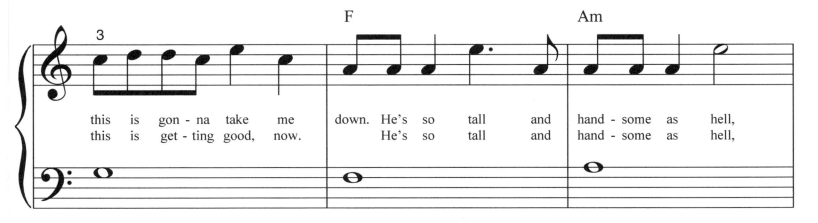

this is gon - na take me down. He's so tall and hand - some as hell,
this is get - ting good, now. He's so tall and hand - some as hell,

he's so bad but he does it so ____ well. ____ I can see the end
he's so bad but he does it so ____ well. ____ And when we've had our

as it be - gins, my one con - di - tion is: ____
ver - y last kiss, my last re - quest ____ is: ____

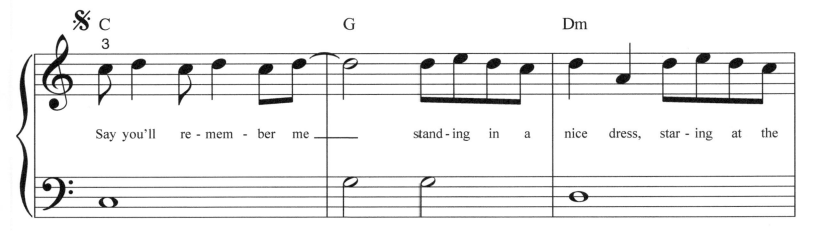

Say you'll re - mem - ber me ____ stand - ing in a nice dress, star - ing at the

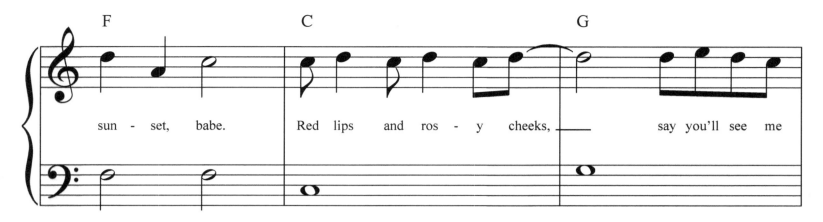

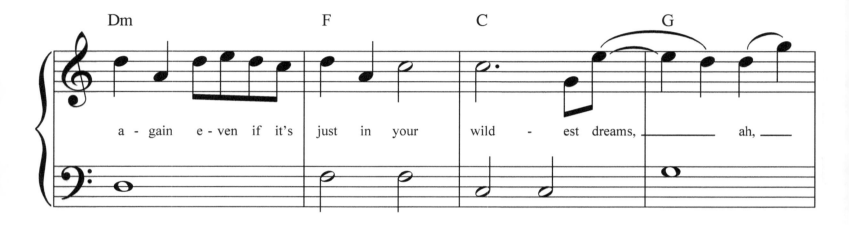

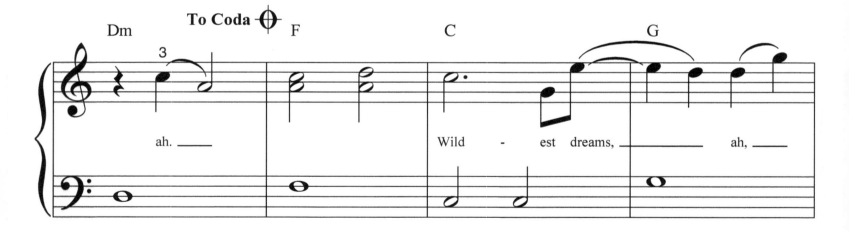

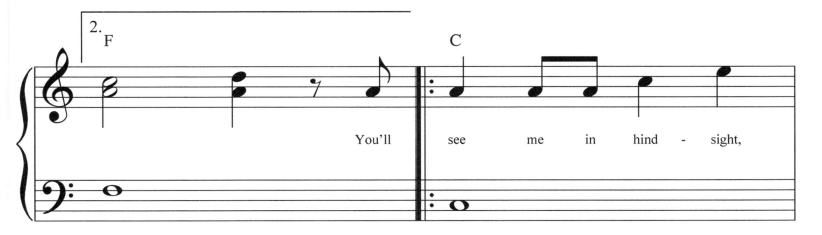

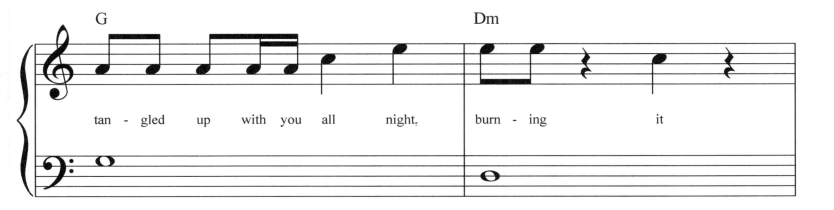

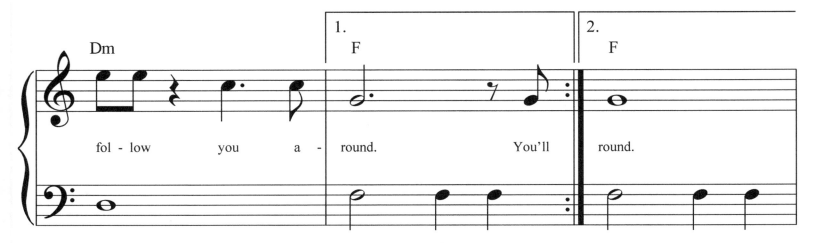

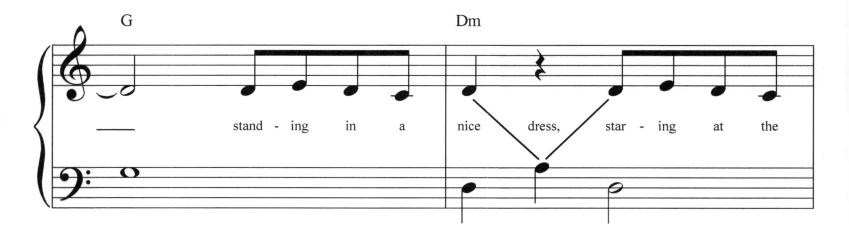

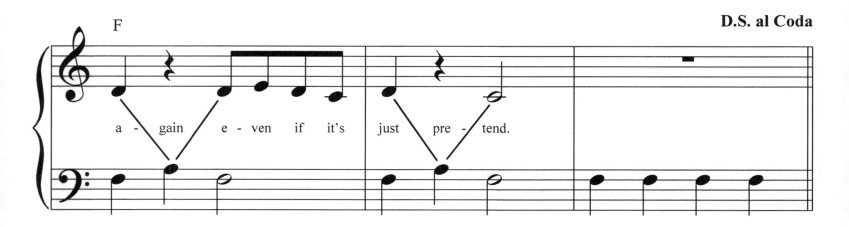

CODA

In your wild - est dreams, _____ ah, _____

ah. E - ven if it's just in your _____ wild - est dreams, _

_____ ah, _____ ah. _____ In _____ your

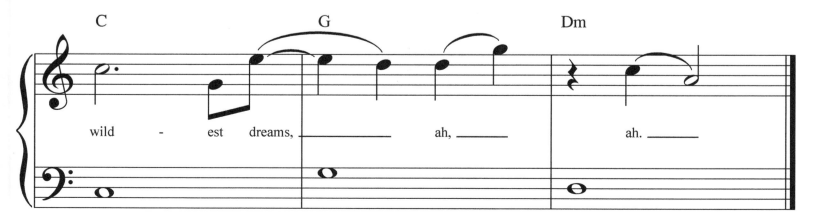

wild - est dreams, _____ ah, _____ ah. _____

HOW YOU GET THE GIRL

Words and Music by TAYLOR SWIFT,
MAX MARTIN and SHELLBACK

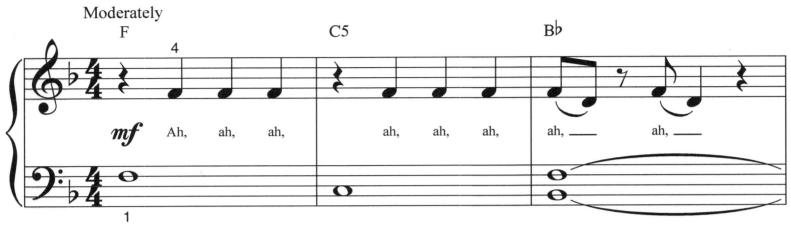

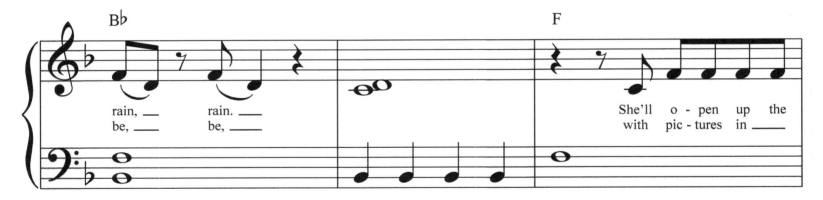

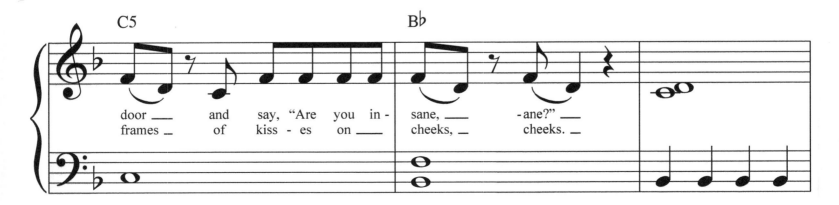

Copyright © 2014 Sony/ATV Music Publishing LLC, Taylor Swift Music and MXM
All Rights on behalf of Sony/ATV Music Publishing LLC and Taylor Swift Music Administered by Sony/ATV Music Publishing LLC, 424 Church Street, Suite 1200, Nashville, TN 37219
All Rights on behalf of MXM Administered Worldwide by Kobalt Songs Music Publishing
International Copyright Secured   All Rights Reserved

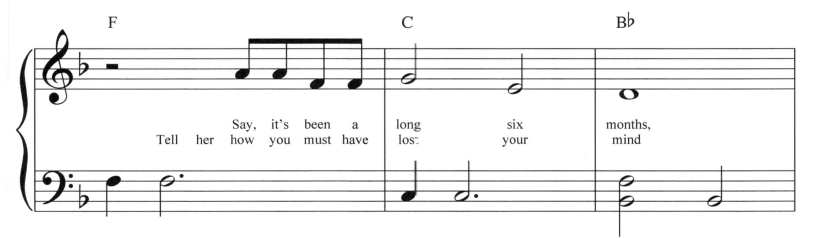

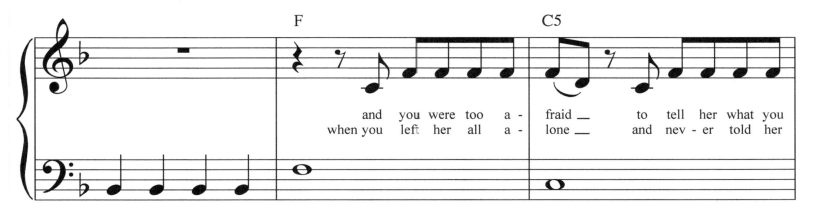

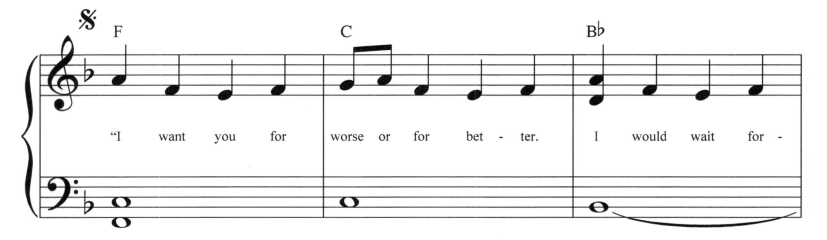

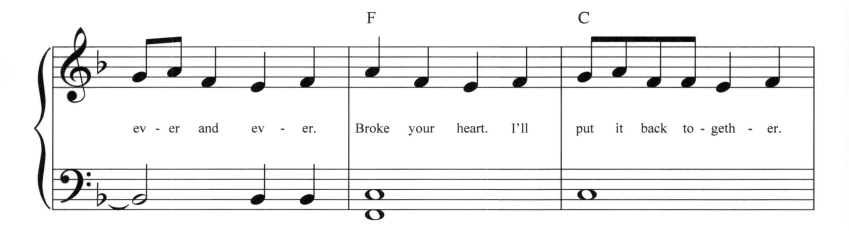

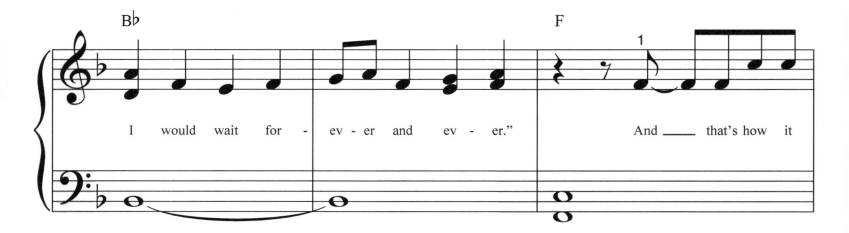

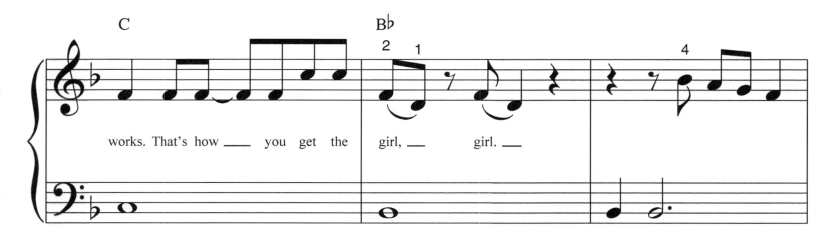

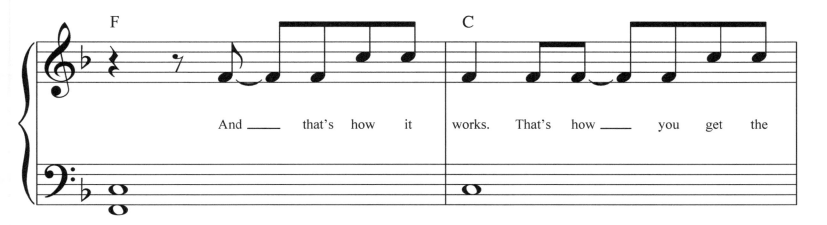

And ____ that's how it works. That's how ____ you get the

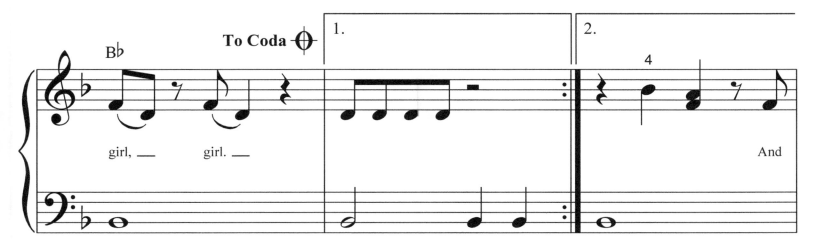

To Coda ⊕ | **1.** | **2.**

girl, ____ girl. ____ And

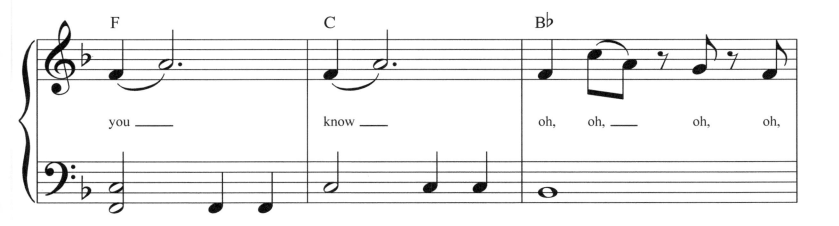

you ____ know ____ oh, oh, ____ oh, oh,

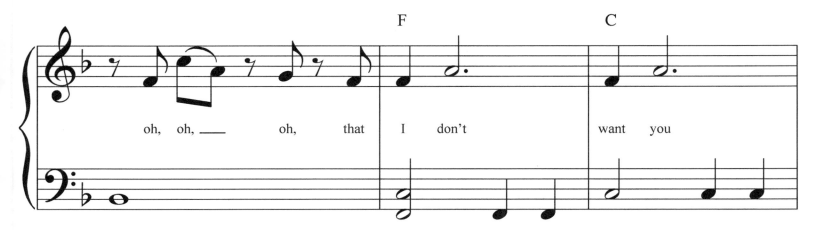

oh, oh, ____ oh, that I don't want you

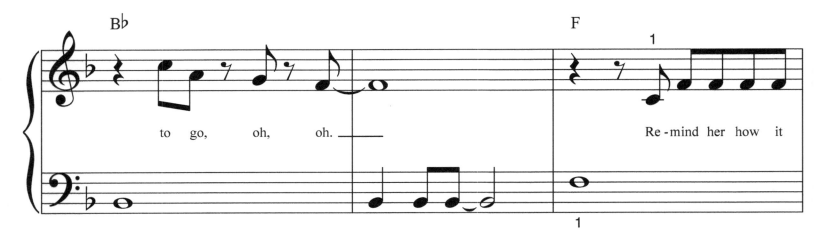

to go, oh, oh. Re-mind her how it

used to be:

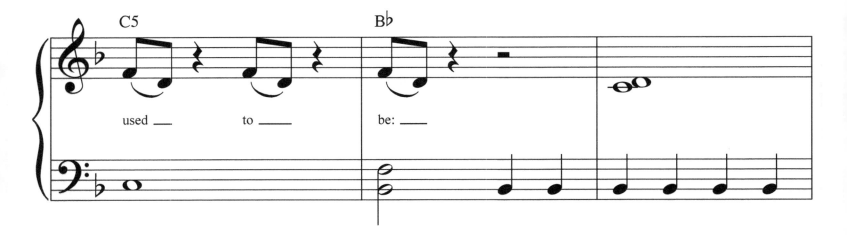

pic-tures in frames of kiss-es on cheeks.

D.S. al Coda

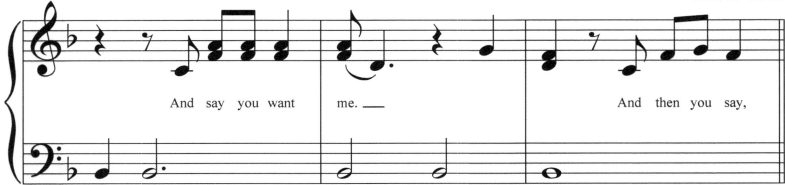

And say you want me. And then you say,

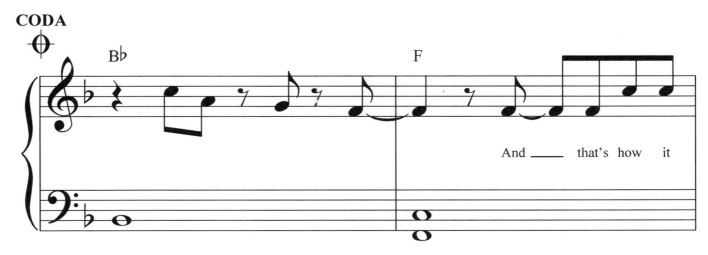

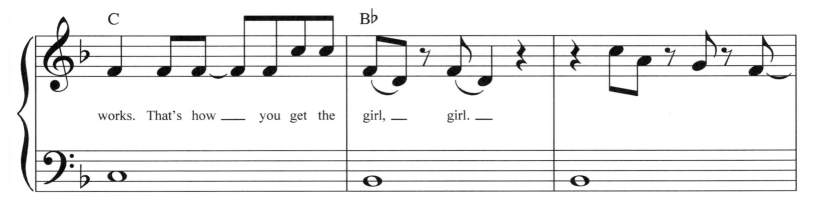

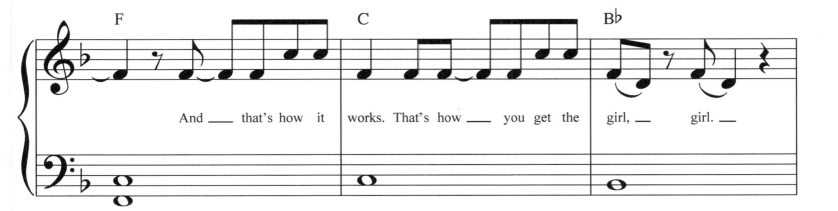

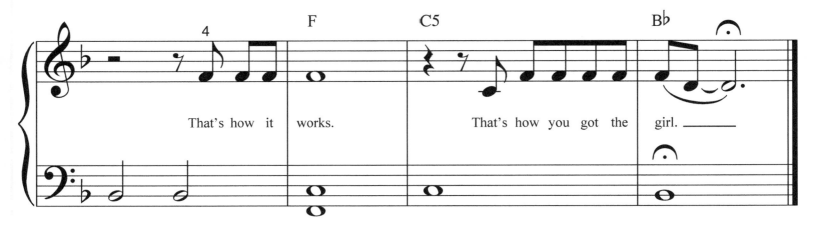

THIS LOVE

Words and Music by
TAYLOR SWIFT

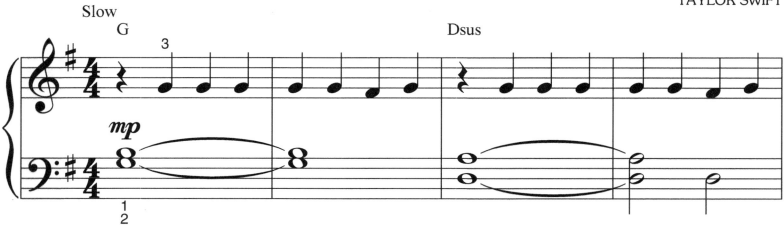

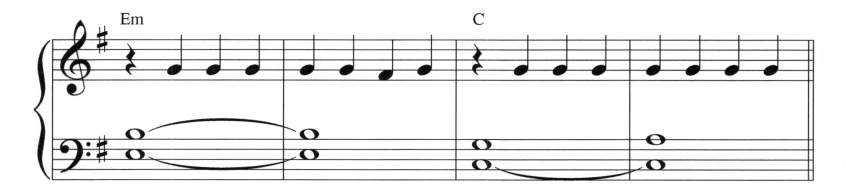

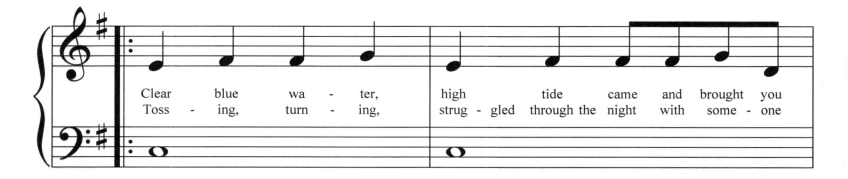

Clear blue wa-ter, high tide came and brought you
Toss-ing, turn-ing, strug-gled through the night with some-one

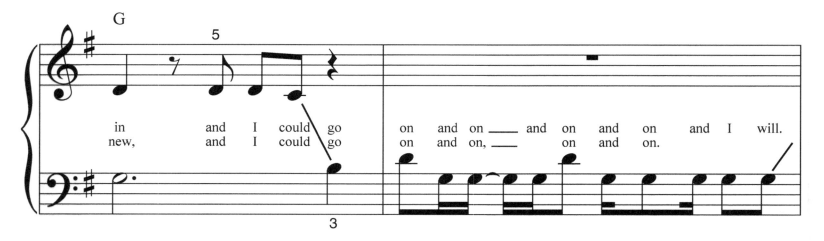

in, and I could go on and on ____ and on and on and I will.
new, and I could go on and on, ____ on and on.

Copyright © 2014 Sony/ATV Music Publishing LLC and Taylor Swift Music
All Rights Administered by Sony/ATV Music Publishing LLC, 424 Church Street, Suite 1200, Nashville, TN 37219
International Copyright Secured   All Rights Reserved

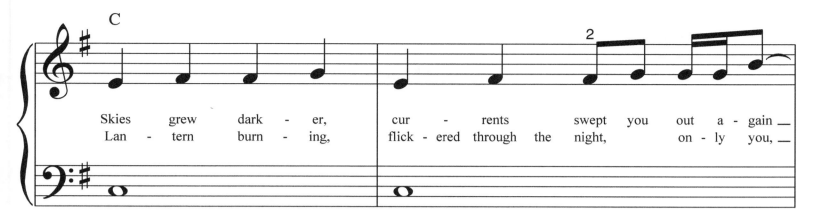

C

Skies grew dark - er, cur - rents swept you out a - gain __
Lan - tern burn - ing, flick - ered through the night, on - ly you, __

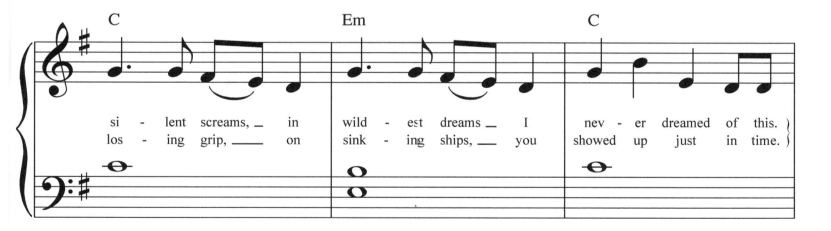

G

__ and you were just gone and gone __ and gone and gone. In __
__ but you are still gone, __ gone, __ gone. In __

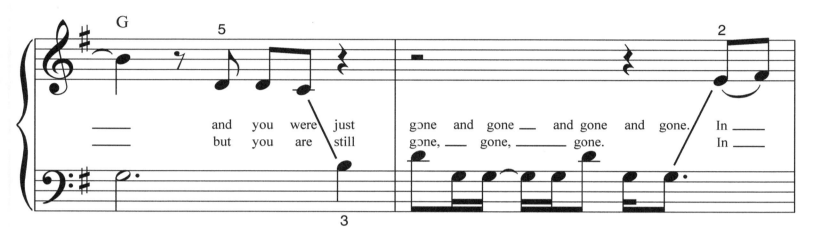

C   Em   C

si - lent screams, __ in wild - est dreams __ I nev - er dreamed of this.
los - ing grip, __ on sink - ing ships, __ you showed up just in time.

G

This love is good, this love is bad, this

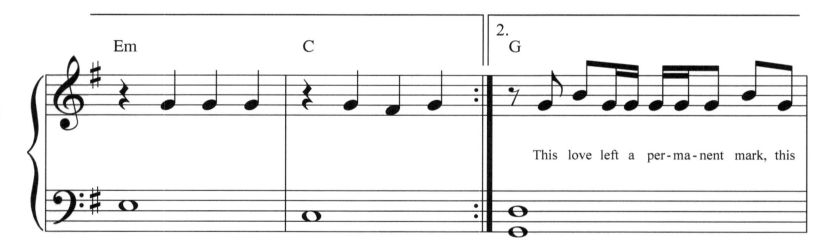

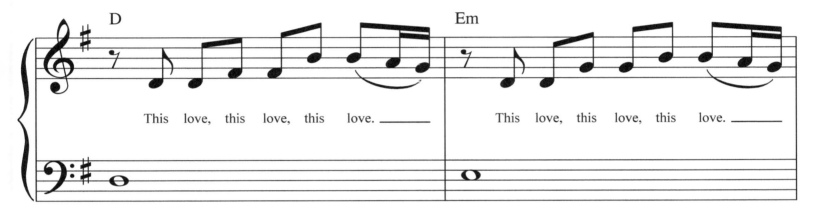

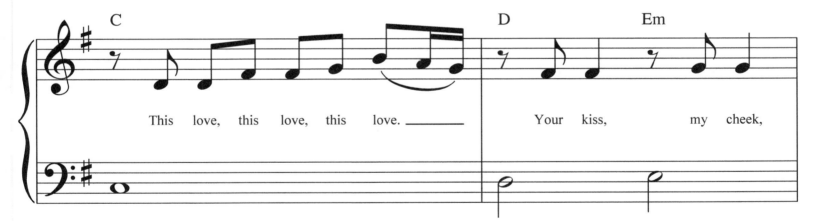

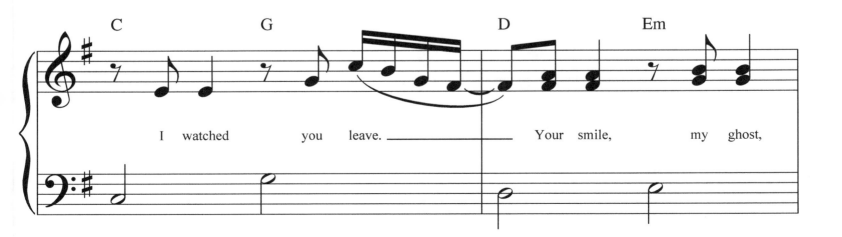

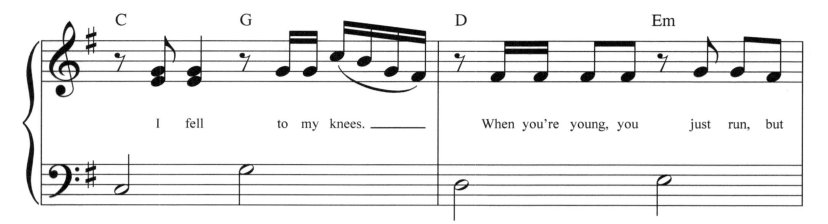

I fell to my knees. _____ When you're young, you just run, but

you come back to what you need. _____ This

love is good, this love is bad, this love is a - live, back from the dead, oh. _____

These hands had to let it go free and this love came back to me, ___ oh. _____

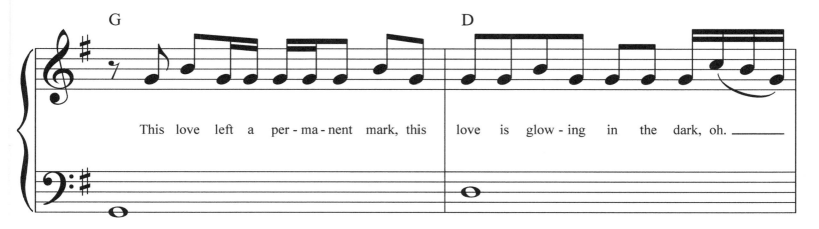

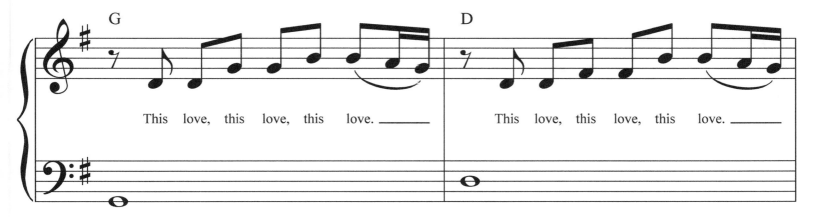

I KNOW PLACES

Words and Music by TAYLOR SWIFT
and RYAN TEDDER

Moderately slow

Copyright © 2014 Sony/ATV Music Publishing LLC, Taylor Swift Music and Write Me A Song Publishing
All Rights on behalf of Sony/ATV Music Publishing LLC and Taylor Swift Music Administered by Sony/ATV Music Publishing LLC, 424 Church Street, Suite 1200, Nashville, TN 37219
All Rights on behalf of Write Me A Song Publishing Administered Worldwide by Kobalt Music Publishing America, Inc.
International Copyright Secured   All Rights Reserved

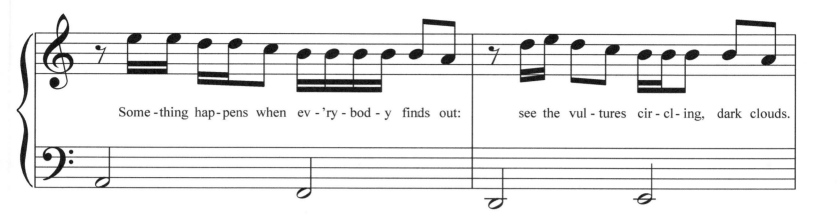

Some-thing hap-pens when ev-'ry-bod-y finds out: see the vul-tures cir-cl-ing, dark clouds.

Love's a frag-ile lit-tle flame, it could burn out, it could burn out. ____ 'Cause

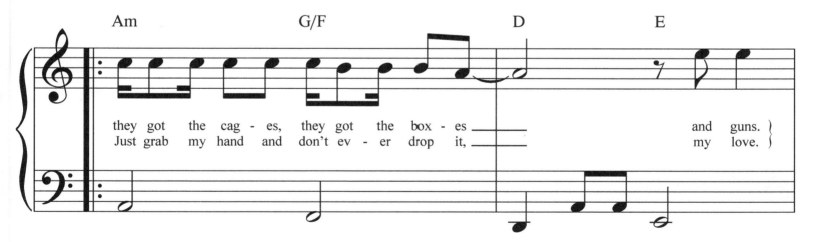

| Am | G/F | D | E |

they got the cag-es, they got the box-es ____ and guns.
Just grab my hand and don't ev-er drop it, ____ my love.

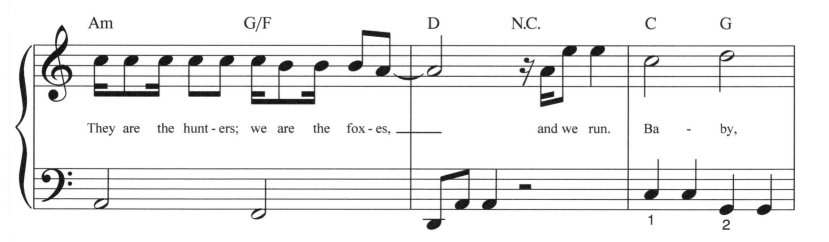

| Am | G/F | D | N.C. | C | G |

They are the hunt-ers; we are the fox-es, ____ and we run. Ba - by,

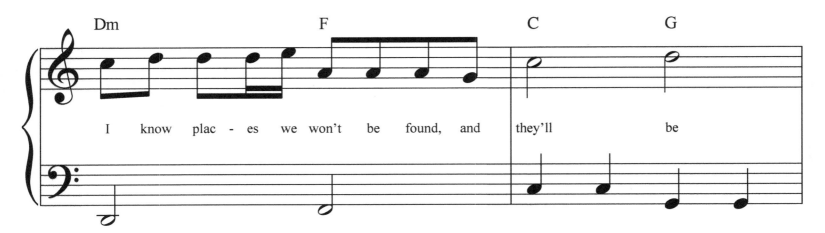

I know plac-es we won't be found, and they'll be

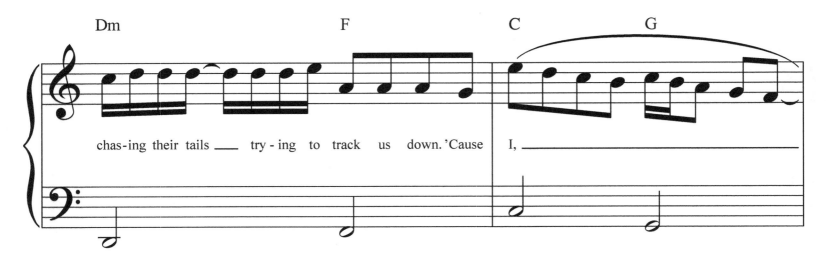

chas-ing their tails ___ try-ing to track us down. 'Cause I, _____

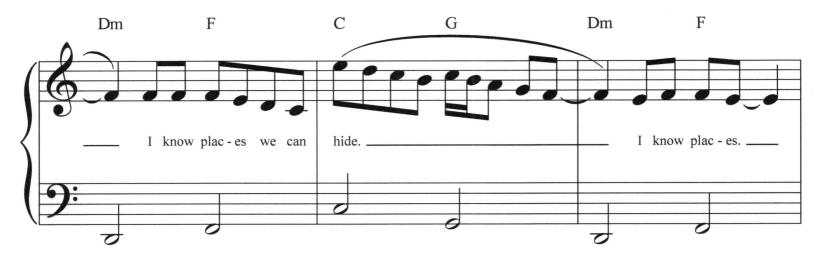

___ I know plac-es we can hide. _____ I know plac-es. ___

I know plac-es. ___ Lights flash and we'll run for the fenc-es.

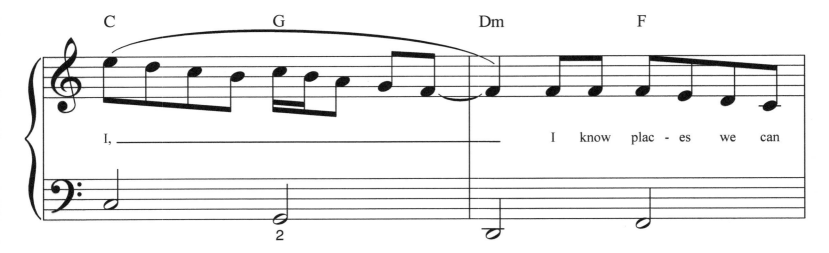

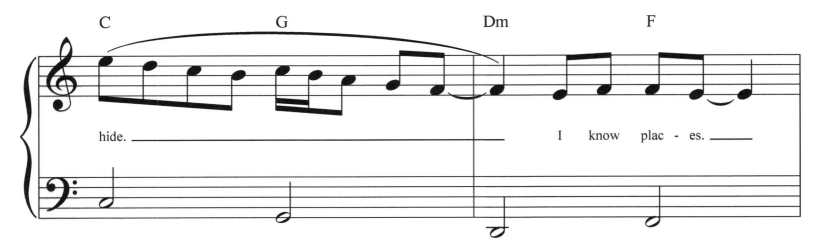

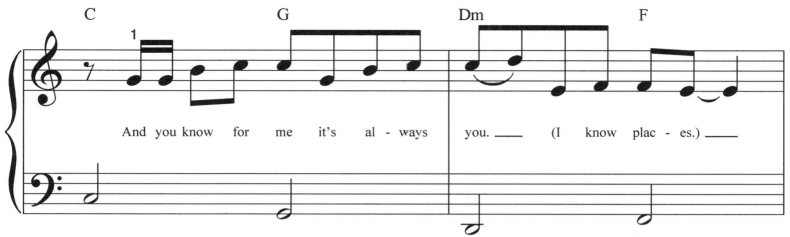

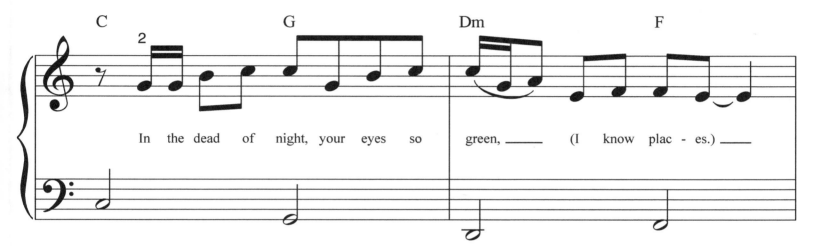

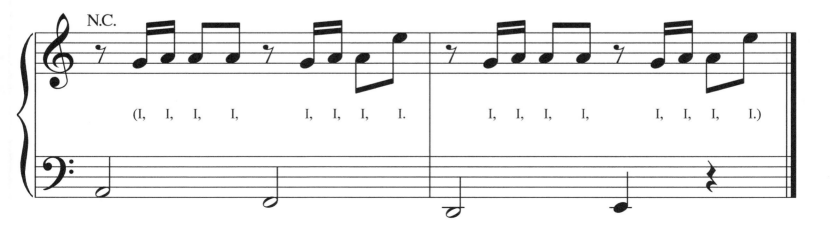

CLEAN

Words and Music by TAYLOR SWIFT
and IMOGEN HEAP

Moderately

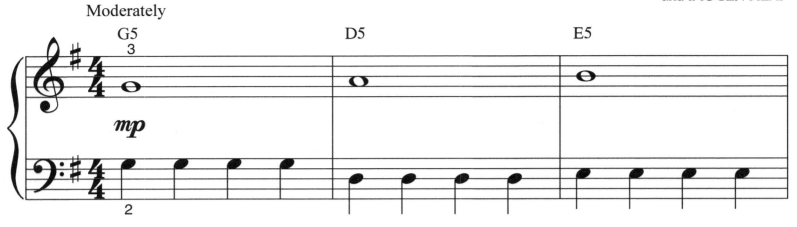

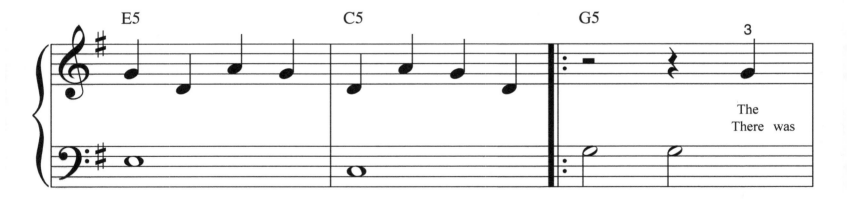

The
There was

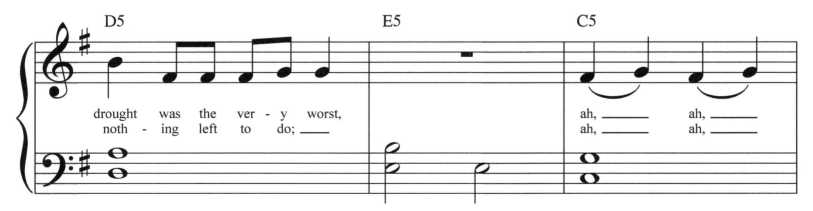

drought was the ver-y worst,
noth-ing left to do; ___

ah, ___ ah, ___
ah, ___ ah,

Copyright © 2014 Sony/ATV Music Publishing LLC, Taylor Swift Music and MXM
All Rights on behalf of Sony/ATV Music Publishing LLC and Taylor Swift Music Administered by Sony/ATV Music Publishing LLC, 424 Church Street, Suite 1200, Nashville, TN 37219
All Rights on behalf of MXM Administered Worldwide by Kobalt Songs Music Publishing
International Copyright Secured   All Rights Reserved

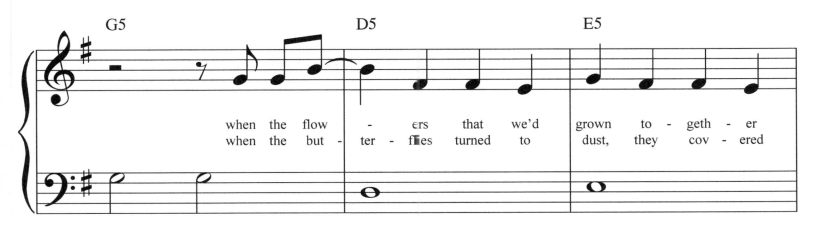

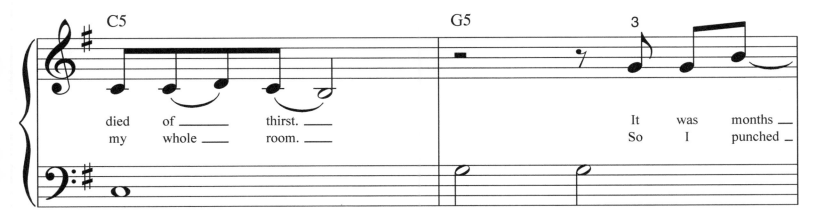

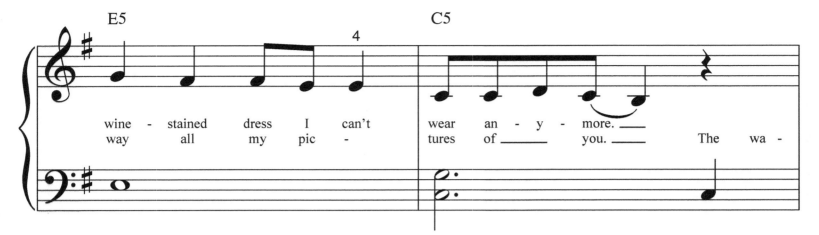

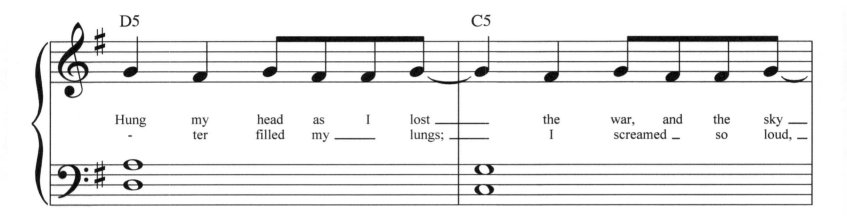

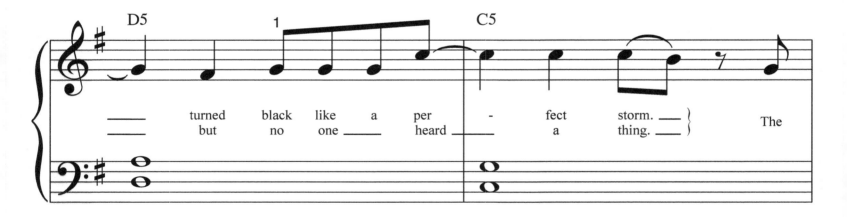

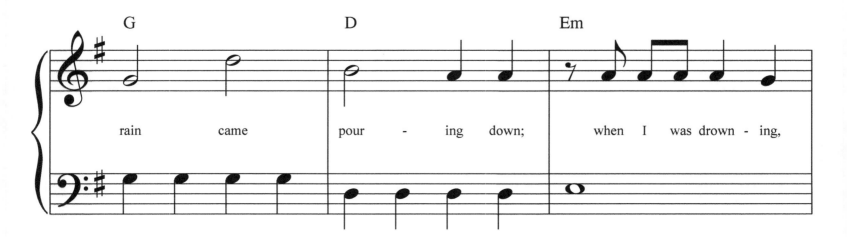

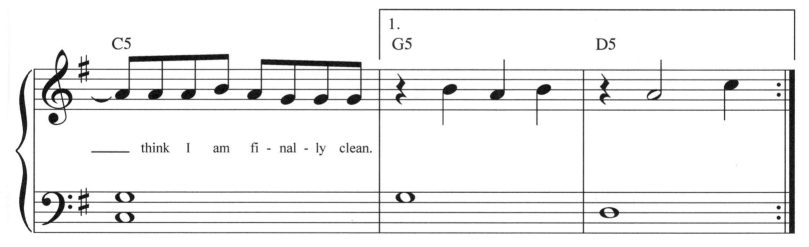

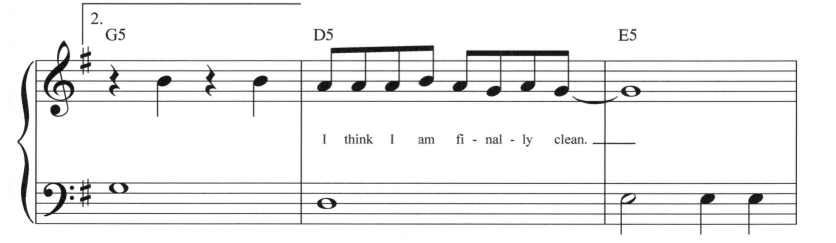

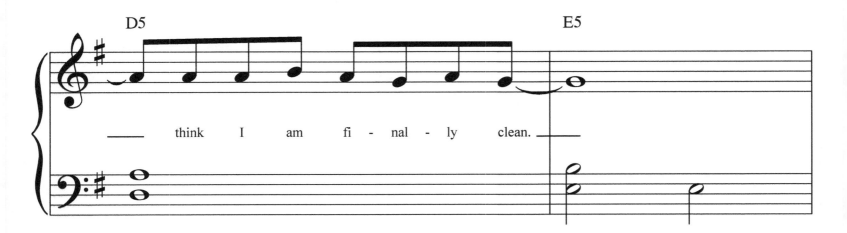

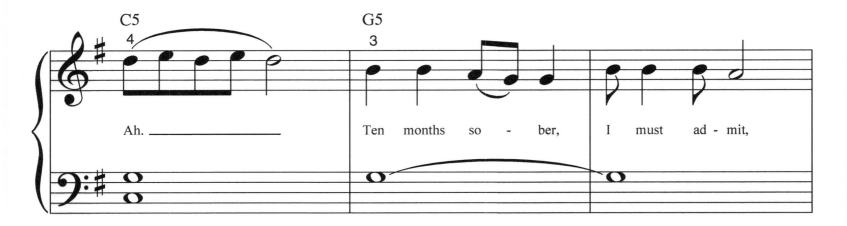

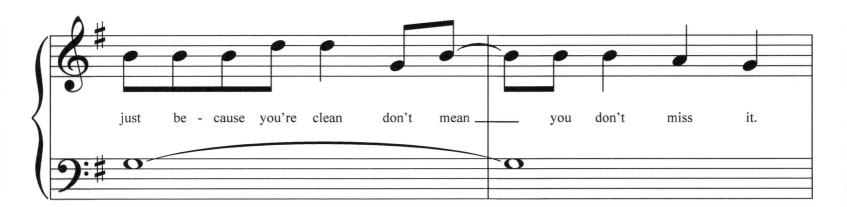

Ten months old - der; I won't give in. Now that I'm clean. I'm nev-

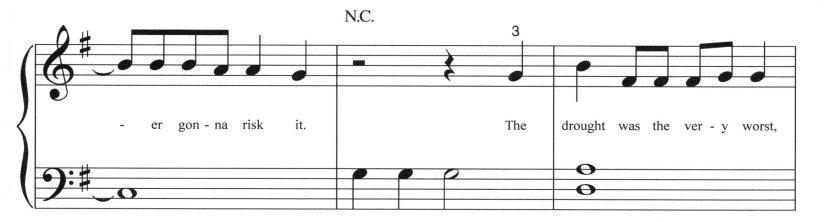

- er gon - na risk it. The drought was the ver - y worst,

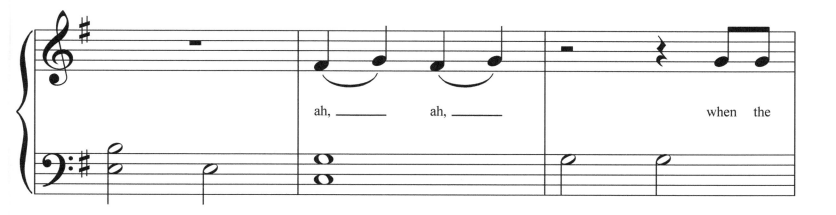

ah, _____ ah, _____ when the

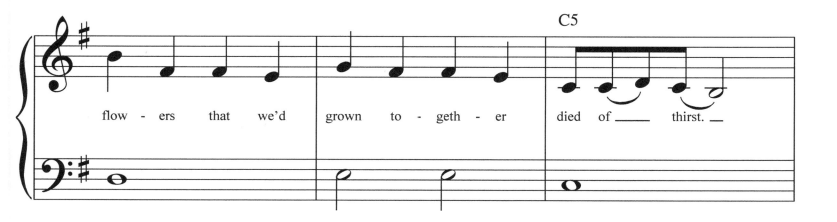

flow - ers that we'd grown to - geth - er died of ___ thirst. __

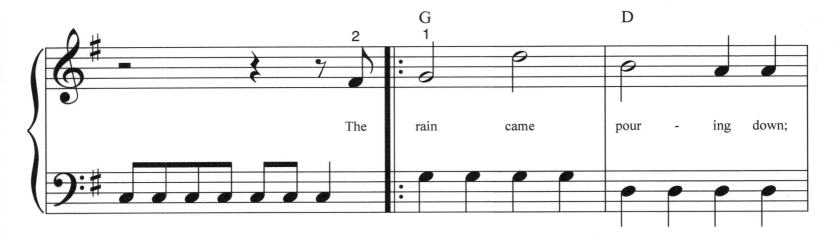

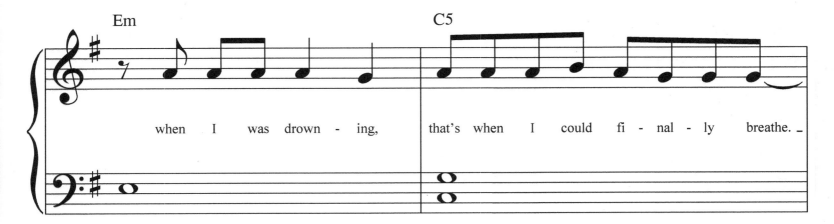

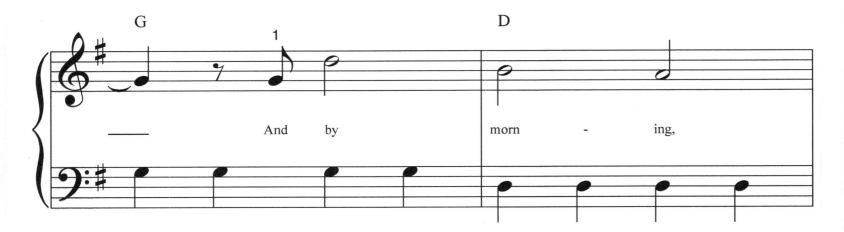

think I am fi - nal - ly clean.

Fi - nal - ly clean.

Think I'm fi - nal - ly clean. Ah, _____ ah. _____

Think I'm fi - nal - ly clean.